Loudoun *County*

BLENDING TRADITION WITH INNOVATION

Written by *Julie Johnson*
Corporate profiles by *Johanna Turner*
Featuring the photography of *David Galen*

Produced in cooperation with the Loudoun County Chamber of Commerce

Credits

Loudoun: Blending Tradition With Innovation

Produced in cooperation with the
Loudoun County Chamber of Commerce

Written by Julie Johnson
Corporate profiles by Johanna Turner
Featuring the photography of David Galen

Community Communications, Inc.
Publishers: Ronald P. Beers and James E. Turner

Staff for *Loudoun: Blending Tradition With Innovation*

Publisher's Sales Associate	*Bill McAllister*
Acquisitions	*Henry S. Beers*
Executive Editor	*James E. Turner*
Editor In Chief	*Wendi Lewis*
Managing Editor	*Lenita Gilreath*
Editorial Consultant	*F. Clifton Berry Jr.*
Design Director	*Scott Phillips*
Designer	*Eddie Lavoie*
Photo Editors	*Eddie Lavoie and Lenita Gilreath*
Production Manager	*Jarrod Stiff*
Contract Manager	*Christi Stevens*
Editorial Assistant	*Amanda Burbank*
Sales Assistant	*Sandra Akers*
Proofreader	*Wynona B. Hall*
Accounting Services	*Sara Ann Turner*
Printing Production	*Gary G. Pulliam*
Prepress and Separations	*Artcraft Graphic Productions*

Community Communications, Inc.
Montgomery, Alabama

James E. Turner, Chairman of the Board
Ronald P. Beers, President
Daniel S. Chambliss, Vice President

CCI

© 2000 Community Communications
All Rights Reserved
Published 2000
Printed in Canada
First Edition
Library of Congress Catalog Number: 00-038415
ISBN Number: 1-58192-016-4

Every effort has been made to ensure the accuracy of the information herein.
However, the authors and Community Communications are not responsible for
any errors or omissions which might have occurred.

Blending Tradition With Innovation

Loudoun

Table of Contents

Foreword, 6
Preface, 8
Bibliography, 130
Enterprise Index, 131
Index, 133-136

Chapter 1
Blending Tradition With Innovation   **10**

Loudoun County offers a quality of life unparalleled in the region. It encompasses a broad spectrum of housing, agriculture, and business. Loudoun's commitment to its heritage, community involvement, and foresight define the character of the county.

Chapter 2
Pride In the Past   **18**

From the early settlers to the Civil War to present day, Loudouners celebrate and preserve the county's heritage. Loudoun's history illustrates its citizens' long-standing record of community activism and reverence for the past.

Chapter 3
Economic Growth and Diversity   **26**

Loudoun County enjoys a strong and diverse economy. Availability of land in a beautiful setting, easy access to Washington Dulles International Airport, and a favorable tax structure enhance the allure of Loudoun's business base.

Chapter 4
A Thriving Downtown Center   **34**

Many of Loudoun County's towns maintain productive and attractive centers, enticing business professionals, retailers, and residents. The area has continued the tradition of small-town life without impeding the flow of progress.

Chapter 5
Cultural Enrichment Abounds   **42**

Cultural and family-oriented activities are plentiful in Loudoun County. The cultural and sporting events complementing the rural backdrop make Loudoun an idyllic destination for residents and visitors alike.

Blending Tradition With Innovation

Chapter 6
Generosity of Spirit   50

Loudoun's community efforts to help those in need are evident in the myriad services offered. Loudoun County has a strong core of volunteers, who strengthen the community through their hard work and generosity.

Chapter 7
Higher Standards of Learning   58

Loudoun's pledge to higher standards of learning and its wide range of educational options draw many families to the county. Loudoun County is among the most rapidly growing school systems in the nation and the fastest growing in Virginia.

Chapter 8
Modern Health Care With An Old-Fashioned Touch   64

Residents are afforded the highest standard of health care and a wide scope of health care services. Community awareness and involvement are the touchstones these facilities use to improve health care services. The health care system in Loudoun utilizes the latest technological advances, while never losing sight of the human aspect of medicine.

Chapter 9
Moving Toward the Future, While Preserving the Past   70

Loudoun County is dedicated to blending tradition with innovation. Loudoun's thoughtful planning creates a thriving economy, committed government body, excellent school system, and a strong community.

Chapter 10
Networks and Technology   76

America Online, Inc., 78-81
United Airlines, 82-83
The Loudoun Times-Mirror, 84-85
Atlantic Coast Airlines, 86-87
TELOS Corporation, 88
Enterworks, Inc., 89
Washington Dulles International Airport, 90
Loudoun County Transportation Association, 91
WAGE, AM 1200, 92

Chapter 11
Professions and Building Loudoun County   94

Merrill Lynch, 96-97
The Miles/LeHane Group, Inc., 98-99
Talbot and Company, Inc., 100-101
Sevila, Saunders, Huddleston & White, 102
Galen Photography, 103

Chapter 12
Business and Finance   104

The Town of Leesburg, Virginia, 106-109
Loudoun County Chamber
   of Commerce, 110-111
Loudoun County Government, 112-113

Chapter 13
Health and Education   114

Loudoun Healthcare, Inc., 116-117
Reston Hospital Center, 118-119
Foxcroft School, 120-121

Chapter 14
The Marketplace   122

Raspberry Falls Golf and Hunt Club, 124-125
The Holiday Inn at Historic
   Carradoc Hall, 126-127
Lansdowne Resort, 128-129

Special thanks to Dulles Marriott Hotel for their participation in this project.

Loudoun

Blending Tradition With Innovation

Foreword

$\mathcal{O}$ver the past decade, the Internet has redefined the way we live, learn, communicate, and work. Through this new medium, hundreds of companies have roared onto the scene—redefining the marketplace, establishing new industries, and creating billions in wealth for America's workers, small investors, and retirees.

Just as the Internet is transforming the global economy, it is also creating a new set of business hubs for this emerging generation of entrepreneurs, investors, inventors, and innovators. In the top tier of those centers of the New Economy is Loudoun County.

Our community and our region have been at the center of the information revolution, and many of the changes that are sweeping the globe are being led by entrepreneurs and companies located right here.

Loudoun County's leadership stems partly from the important businesses that have been established in this area—from Internet backbone and content providers to software and systems engineering. In addition, Loudoun has tremendous nonphysical assets: A vibrant entrepreneurial culture. A federal government that invests heavily in research and development. A well-trained high-tech workforce. First-rate regional universities. And a large and growing base of venture capital.

But just as important as those business considerations are the quality-of-life issues that make Loudoun County such a great place to live and raise a family. The area offers open country spaces and a variety of housing alternatives, excellent schools, transportation, and recreational areas, as well as easy access to Washington, D.C., and the convenience of Washington Dulles International Airport for business and personal travel.

America Online first decided to move its main facilities to Loudoun County in 1996 to take advantage of these many resources, and it has not been disappointed. In just over three years, its workforce in Loudoun County has grown from 425 to over 3,500, and it has expanded its campus from a single building to five, with two more under construction.

AOL is thriving in part because of the support Loudoun County provides to the business community. Loudoun has become a magnet for attracting innovative and dynamic businesses to the area, spurring the exchange of ideas, shared problem-solving to regional issues, and continuous innovation.

AOL is pleased to be a part of this vibrant region, which blends the best of tradition with a community of innovative companies and people for a better future. As we enter the Internet Century, AOL is proud to call Loudoun County home.

—*Steve Case*
CEO of America Online

7

Preface

Loudoun County is my home. The rural beauty, people, and opportunities make the county a unique and interesting place to live and work. For me, it symbolizes the American Dream.

Upon settling in Loudoun, I immediately felt at home as neighbors, local officials, retailers, and business professionals offered friendship, encouragement, and support. During my research, I met many members of the community, each with a story to tell and a desire to express why Loudoun is special to them.

I'd like to thank the Chamber for their support in this project. I'd also like to express my gratitude to the people of Loudoun County for their dedication to the community and their willingness to share their experiences and knowledge.

—*Julie Johnson*
Author

Fields of brilliantly colored flowers make their presence known along Loudoun's country roads. It is this breathtaking natural beauty that residents and tourists find so intoxicating. Photo by David Galen.

Blending Tradition With Innovation

Loudoun

Chapter One

Blending Tradition With Innovation

From the Blue Ridge Mountains to the Potomac River, Loudoun offers a breathtaking view of a county proud of its heritage, dedicated to community, and innovative in its approach to progress.

◣

The appeal of its pastoral beauty has lured many to call Loudoun home. Lovettsville, which rests in the northern portion of the county on the Potomac River, continues its farming tradition and generally remains unaffected by development. Its vantage point on the Maryland-Virginia border is becoming attractive to commuters working in suburban Maryland and D.C. Photo by David Galen.

The vast majority of land in Loudoun County remains a viable farming commodity. More than 200,000 acres are farmed in the tradition of the county's forefathers. Photo by David Galen.

Nestled between the foothills of the Blue Ridge Mountains and the banks of the Potomac River, 35 miles northwest of Washington, D.C., Loudoun County epitomizes the American dream. The county offers a quality of life unparalleled in the region. Its more than 300,000 acres encompass a broad spectrum of housing, agriculture, and business, and the community's involvement in preserving the aesthetic quality of the county is evident in the approximately 30,000 acres it has apportioned as public or open space.

Two-thirds of land in the county remains a viable farming commodity. More than 200,000 acres are farmed in traditional and modern ways. The appeal of its pastoral beauty has lured many to call Loudoun home. Over the past decade, Loudoun has seen tremendous residential development. Housing options vary greatly in the county's residential areas. The home buyer is offered everything from town homes and apartments to antebellum mansions, contemporary center hall colonials, and secluded estates with large tracts of land. Homeowners are vigilant in maintaining their properties.

Many of these residents are employees of the burgeoning number of corporations conducting business in the county. These corporations have positively influenced the direction in which the county is moving. As a result of corporate titans such as America Online ensconcing their headquarters firmly in Loudoun, the scope of real estate, education, health care, and the economy is evolving. Other major employers in Loudoun include United Airlines, MCI WorldCom, Atlantic Coast Airlines, Telos Corporation, Lansdowne Resort, Xerox Document University, and others. These corporations contribute to a stable economy, support educational programs and health facilities, enhance the value of real estate, and encourage efficient planning of the area's transportation systems.

With the rapid growth has come the construction of many state-of-the-art schools. In the 1999-2000 school year, Loudoun enrolled more than 30,000 students in its schools. By the year 2005, Loudoun will have commenced or completed construction on 20 additional schools for its students. Loudoun County is the fastest-growing school system in the state and the 11th-largest public school system in Virginia.

Along with a healthy corporate environment is a robust tourism industry. Loudoun County boasts an abundance of attractions that intrigue, delight,

Blending Tradition With Innovation

and surprise visitors. The county welcomes tourists to repose in one of more than 18 charming bed-and-breakfasts or relax in the modern amenities available at more than one dozen hotels and a premier resort.

Tourists will find an interesting mix of towns and villages throughout Loudoun County. Each has its own distinct character and history. The passage of time is clearly evident in several towns, while in many of the smaller villages time seems to stand still.

Aldie's diminutive size enhances its charm. The village lies to the east of its well-known neighbor, Middleburg. Aldie Mill, erected in 1796, is a charmingly restored five-story mill currently functioning as a museum. The village is the site of a major cavalry fight during the Civil War.

Arcola is located on the southeastern perimeter of the county. This former coach stop shares close proximity to Washington Dulles International Airport. Despite its location, Arcola remains a tiny and tranquil village.

The county's tremendous growth is apparent in Ashburn. Located in the eastern portion of the county, Ashburn was once a small community comprised of less than 100 families. The original downtown, known as Old Ashburn, was a regular stop for the Washington and Old Dominion Railroad. Today, Ashburn entices citizens to its planned communities. These communities include sporting facilities, shopping centers, recreational lakes, town homes, and single-family dwellings. Two of the more notable communities are Ashburn Village and Ashburn Farm.

Bluemont, formerly known as Snickersville, enjoys spectacular vistas of the Blue Ridge Mountains. On the fringes of western Loudoun, Bluemont's cool mountain breezes and secluded, heavily wooded lots have provided summer respite to urban dwellers for years. Mount Weather, a weather station operated by the Federal Emergency Management Agency, is tucked in the southern portion of Bluemont and yields astounding views in its own right. The town's population swells considerably in September, as visitors take pleasure in the antiques, crafts, delicacies, and bluegrass and country music at the Bluemont Fair.

Hamilton's primary function as a stagecoach stop does not overshadow the period of growth it experienced in the late nineteenth century with the introduction of the Washington and Old Dominion Railroad. Once known as Harmony, Hamilton is located approximately seven miles west of Leesburg.

The unique architecture abiding throughout Loudoun County is well represented in the northwestern town of Hillsboro. This tiny hamlet, studded with stone buildings and walls, is a still life of nineteenth-century Loudoun. Homes have been lovingly restored and the countryside is virtually untouched.

Leesburg is the crossroad of Loudoun County. Twelve miles northwest of Washington-Dulles International Airport, Leesburg

Many area residents are employees of a burgeoning number of corporations conducting business in the county. These corporations have positively influenced the direction in which Loudoun is moving. Photo by David Galen.

Middleburg borders Fauquier County in the southern portion of Loudoun. Despite skirmishes during the Civil War, Middleburg has emerged as a gentrified and prosperous village. The Red Fox Inn is an eighteenth-century bed-and-breakfast, one of several picturesque bed-and-breakfast inns in the county. Photo by David Galen.

Loudoun

(opposite) Pictured is just one of the many farms enhancing the pastoral beauty and charm of Loudoun County. Photo by David Galen.

(right) Towns such as Airmont, Bluemont, and Philomont are finding a genuine need and want for the old-fashioned general store. The ambiance found in these markets recalls an era when patrons shopped for staples and caught up on local news. Photo by David Galen.

(below) The unique architecture abiding throughout Loudoun County is well represented in the northwestern town of Hillsboro—a still life of nineteenth-century Loudoun. Photo by David Galen.

is the seat of government for Loudoun County and a hub for tourists visiting the western and eastern portions of the county. Leesburg's population has grown steadily in recent years. Originally known as George Town, Leesburg was renamed in honor of Virginia's prominent Lee family. Today, the community is a thriving mix of business and tourism.

Despite its larger population, Leesburg has been successful in sustaining its small-town charm.

Located south of Purcellville, Lincoln was settled in 1745 by Pennsylvanian Quakers. The only active Quaker meeting house in Virginia resides in Lincoln.

Lovettsville rests in the northern portion of the county on the Potomac River. Lovettsville was settled by Germans in 1732 and was at one time known as New Town. Its current name is derived from Lovett family members who subdivided property and sold lots. The town continues its farming tradition and generally remains unaffected by development. Its vantage point on the Maryland-Virginia border is becoming attractive to commuters working in suburban Maryland and D.C.

North of Leesburg, Lucketts has become renowned for its summer fair, which attracts visitors from all corners of the county and beyond. The community has a history dating to the Piscataway Indians, who inhabited the region for thousands of years. Presently, this small town is dotted with farms, roadside antiques, and a strong and active community center.

Middleburg borders Fauquier County in the southern portion of Loudoun. Established in 1787, it is the quintessence of horse country. As the heart of thoroughbred horse breeding and foxhunting in Virginia, breeders and riders alike have come to Middleburg to indulge in their love of horses. Despite skirmishes during the Civil War, Middleburg has emerged as a gentrified and prosperous village.

Tucked in the northwestern pocket of the county, tiny Neersville maintains a one-room schoolhouse.

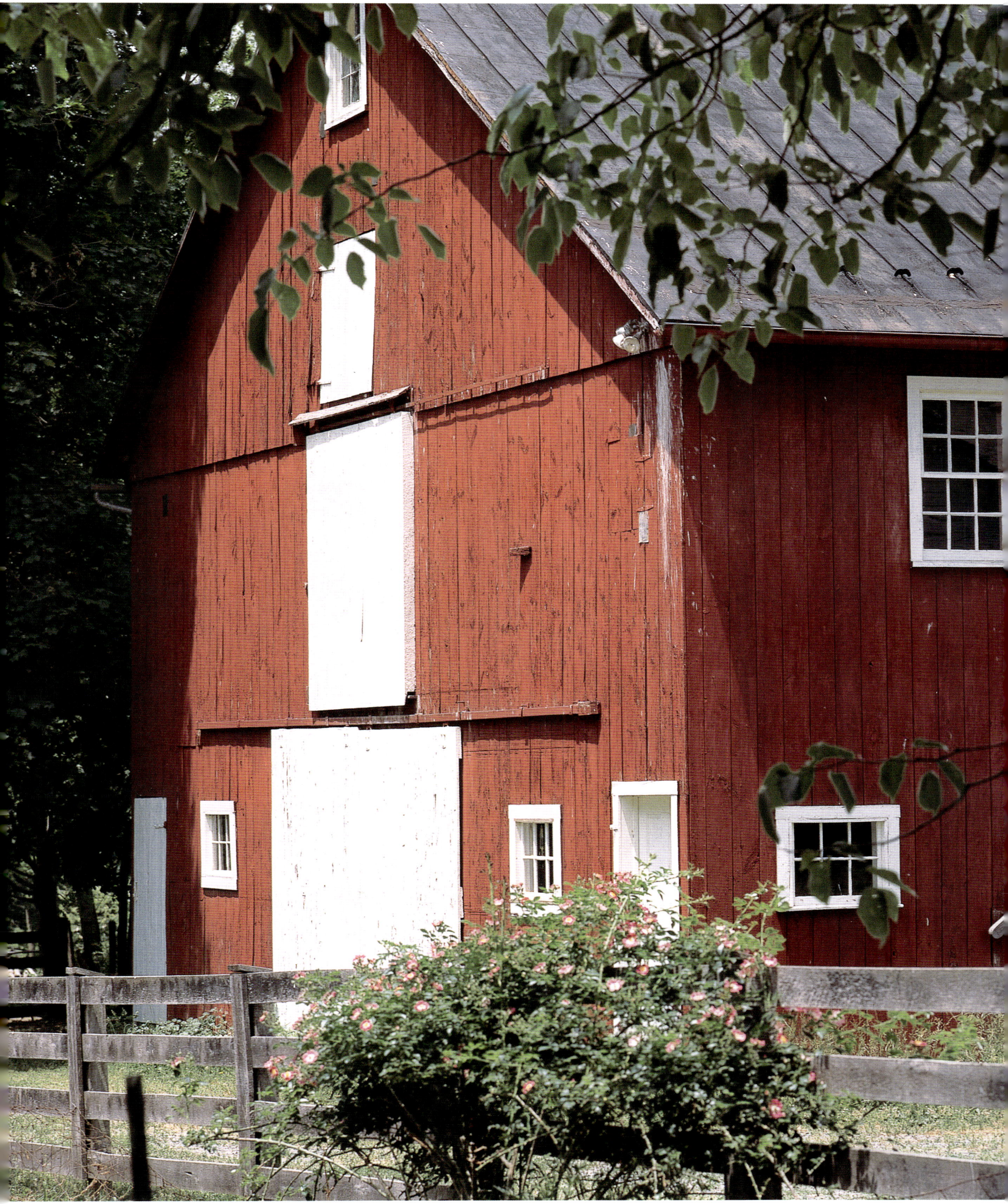

South Riding, a newly established residential development located south of Washington Dulles International Airport, is attracting many commuters seeking good property values and convenience to Washington, D.C. Photo by David Galen.

Paeonian Springs sits squarely between Waterford and Leesburg. Established in 1890, its name suggests its most well-known resource. The natural springs once touted as medicinal are now purely aesthetic. Long before it was fashionable, the area exported bottled water throughout the country. Like many areas with access to natural springs, Paeonian Springs once thrived as a resort at the turn of the century.

Philomont is in the southwestern corner of Loudoun County and remains a quaint and relatively undisturbed village. Visitors out for a Sunday drive will appreciate this engaging spot and encompassing farmland.

West of Leesburg, Purcellville rests in the heart of rich agricultural land in the Loudoun Valley. The town's population is growing rapidly, and local officials are resolute in preserving its rural beauty. Franklin Park is a newly established 203-acre recreational facility for county residents.

Incorporated in 1900 and named for a 910-foot-high hill, Round Hill's elevation played a significant role in the Civil War as a reconnaissance point for both Union and Confederate armies. Round Hill lies northeast of Bluemont in western Loudoun. Its peripheral view of the Loudoun Valley and the Blue Ridge Mountains, as well as its convenience to transportation, contributes to the residential growth it has seen in recent years.

South Riding and Broadlands are newly established residential developments located near Washington Dulles International Airport. Like Sterling, they are attracting many commuters seeking good property values and convenience to Washington, D.C.

Sterling lies in the southeastern corridor of the county. It was home to several of the county's dairy farms. More than a century old, Sterling has reinvented itself as a desirable residential area for commuters and a growing retail and corporate

Blending Tradition With Innovation

environment. Sterling has developed several successful planned communities, including Cascades, Countryside, and Lowes Island.

Like most of the villages in the northern portion of the county, Taylorstown remains a bucolic setting. Settled by Quakers and Germans in 1734, Taylorstown enjoys an unhurried existence. The villagers have renovated a substantial number of homes.

Much of Waterford has been shaped by its strong Quaker roots. Settled in 1733 and approximately nine miles northwest of Leesburg, Waterford has faced its own adversity throughout the years. Opposition to slavery and the Civil War literally pitted brother against brother and neighbor against neighbor in several instances. To its credit, Waterford has paid homage to its history through the highly dedicated Waterford Foundation. Each year, the Waterford Foundation honors the fine craftsmanship of its Quaker ancestors with the Homes Tour and Craft Exhibit. This event is more than 50 years old and draws over 30,000 visitors to partake in festivities including Civil War reenactments, self-guided tours of historical homes, hundreds of artisans, music, and other special events. Unlike other national landmark villages, Waterford is a thriving community where residents conduct business and pleasure amid the beauty and tradition of the past.

Loudoun County's devotion to tradition, community activism, and thoughtful planning for the future define the unique character of the region. The county invites a sense of belonging through its beauty, diversity, history, and deeply satisfying culture. Opportunities appear limitless and ever changing within the county, yet citizens, businesses, and local officials are sensitive to Loudoun's historical significance and magnificent landscape. Loudoun's support of community activism lends itself to the intoxicating mixture of tradition and innovation it sees today. Loudouners remain reverent to the past while embracing the future. This ideology, derived from the motto on Lord Loudoun's own coat of arms, "Byde My Time," will give the county strength as it enters the twenty-first century and beyond.

Loudoun County is enjoying a resurgence in the country store. Several stores have been renovated recently. A few stores also invite visitors to stop at their roadside stands. Photo by David Galen.

Loudoun

Blending Tradition With Innovation

Chapter Two

Pride in the Past

Pride in Loudoun County's history runs deep. While Loudoun has played an instrumental role throughout our country's history, the personal repercussions of these events have shaped the Loudoun of today.

One of the county's more prominent Civil War memorials is Ball's Bluff Regional Park. The battle of Ball's Bluff, fought on the banks of the Potomac River, proved to be a key victory for the Confederates. Photo by David Galen.

Loudoun's natural beauty and rural atmosphere enticed Franklin Delano Roosevelt to summer at Oatlands Plantation. Photo by David Galen.

Loudoun is acutely aware of the importance of preserving the landscape. Local government, preservationists, historians, and residents work earnestly to find creative and cost-effective solutions to growth and conservation. Photo by David Galen.

Although much emphasis is placed on the county's connection to the Civil War, Loudoun has been inhabited for more than 12,000 years. Bands of nomads were known to roam the region in search of big game animals such as bison. Several sectors of American Indians settled throughout Loudoun. The Manahoac tribe lived in the western portion of the county, while the Algonkians inhabited the east. The Iroquois were also known to frequent the area, as were several other tribes in the islands of the Potomac River. Many of these tribes traveled between the Carolinas and New York in the region now known as Route 15. With the signing of the Treaty of Albany in 1722, the American Indians migrated west of the Blue Ridge, which is present-day Loudoun's western boundary. Soon after their migration, the county's early settlers arrived and established themselves in the area.

In 1757, Loudoun was established from Fairfax territory, and the Virginia Assembly officially organized the county. Loudoun's auspicious name derives from the fourth earl of Loudoun, John Campbell. A Scottish nobleman, Lord Loudoun served as the British Armed Forces' commander-in-chief in North America during the early years of the county. Loudoun's honorary title as governor of Virginia from 1756 to 1768 sealed the county's name.

Loudoun's cultural diversity began as early as 1725, when English from the Tidewater region settled in eastern Loudoun. These English settlers often came from titled nobility and were granted land in this portion of the county. They cultivated tobacco on their plantations and frequently maintained large numbers of slaves. The Scotch-Irish traveled through the county on their way to the Carolinas, but a small faction did settle in Loudoun. Germans inhabited Lovettsville and its surrounding areas, usually in close proximity to the Quakers. Large numbers of Quakers established themselves in Waterford and present-day Lincoln.

One cannot overlook Loudoun's significance in the American Revolutionary War. In addition to many of Loudoun's own men enlisting in the fight against the British, Loudoun voters passed the Loudoun Resolves to denounce British taxation and protect the rights and liberties of its citizens.

Interestingly, the early settlers came from varied backgrounds. Not all farmers and plantation owners were wealthy slave owners. Many small farmers held no slaves and Quakers disapproved of slavery. Many of the German settlers also opposed slavery

Blending Tradition With Innovation

August Court Days, sponsored by the Loudoun Restoration and Preservation Society, celebrates colonial Loudoun. Photo by David Galen.

and sided with Union sentiments during the Civil War. Despite the county, as well as the state, being predominantly Confederate, Waterford had an organized Union force among its residents. Virginia was considered a border state, and since Loudoun was located in the northern section of the state, it was home to a number of Union sympathizers. These early settlers have influenced Loudoun's present landscape. Tobacco farming blighted the fertile land in the east, while in the west, Quakers, Germans, and Scotch-Irish tilled the soil into a lush valley of undulating farmland.

Architecturally, the German and Quaker influence is apparent in the many homes and buildings in and around Waterford, Taylorstown, Lovettsville, and Lincoln.

During the next century, the county grew steadily. Mills and agriculture prospered with the dawning of the Industrial Age. Loudoun County became a milling center with nearly 70 mills in the area. These mills were the center of daily business as well as local gossip.

As North and South fought, Loudoun became a microcosm of the Civil War. Embroiled in the

Loudoun

midst of battle, civil unrest among residents was more strongly felt as brothers and neighbors skirmished over secession and slavery. One of the county's more prominent Civil War memorials is Ball's Bluff Regional Park. This battle, fought on the banks of the Potomac River, proved to be a key victory for the Confederates. The site is the final resting place for more than 50 Union soldiers. All but one soldier are unknown.

Physically, Loudoun's battle scars can be seen in the countryside. During November of 1864, burning raids severely marred the Loudoun Valley. Rich farmland and mills were torched and livestock pilfered in an attempt to find Colonel John Mosby and his raiders. Mosby and his men used their knowledge of the area to evade Union captors. This path of destruction intersected the Appalachian Trail in the western part of the county. This trail is a visual reminder of the county's abundant history and spectacular landscape. Despite devastation to their property, residents remained steadfast in their silence of Mosby's whereabouts. Battles aside, the sheer volume of soldiers advancing through the county on their way to Antietam in 1862 and then again to Gettysburg in 1863 laid waste to the unblemished landscape. Situated between the Union capital of Washington, D.C., and the Confederate capital of Richmond, Loudoun became a thoroughfare for passing troops. Wagons, soldiers, and horses rolled through towns such as Leesburg, leaving little in their wake. Control of Loudoun vacillated between Confederate and Union hands with little discord, due, in part, to its pocket of Union sympathizers and reputation as a border state.

While preserving tradition, Loudoun was and continues its history of forward thinking. In 1865, the towns of Leesburg and Middleburg established Freedman's Bureau. The bureau provided guidance to newly freed slaves who were lacking educations, jobs, and homes. The creation and success of this organization, along with its eventual federal branch, contributed to the diversity and strength of the county.

Loudoun's long-standing record of excellence in education began in 1870, when the county opened

Residents and visitors can enjoy theatrical productions as well as house and garden tours at the historic Oatlands Mansion. Photo by David Galen.

An elegant domain, Whitehall Estate is now owned by a catering company. Photo by David Galen.

its doors to public education. Today, the scope of education has expanded and continues to strive for excellence.

The quiet dignity of Loudoun led prominent World War II General George C. Marshall and his wife to call it home in 1941. General Marshall holds a special place in the hearts of the county's residents. Loudouners exemplify the integrity, diligence, and humility he brought to the Marshall Plan, which rebuilt Europe's economy after World War II. His spirit presides over the town of Leesburg, where a statue bears his likeness, and his home, Dodona Manor, continues to watch over this vital community.

Loudoun has long appealed to the country's political leaders. Several secretaries of state have made their home in Loudoun, and former Virginia Governor Westmoreland Davis cherished his farm of more than 1,200 acres in Leesburg. He and Mrs. Davis bequeathed their estate and its contents to the Westmoreland Davis Foundation. It is now known as Morven Park and is the site of many annual events.

With the introduction of Washington Dulles International Airport came a resurgence in the county's population. Constructed in 1962, Dulles has become the gateway to the county and has greatly influenced Loudoun, both historically and economically. Since its debut, the county has created a solid and efficient infrastructure. Dulles's role as an axis to business travelers has created a new and exciting high-tech industry in the region. Major technology corporations are designating Loudoun as their corporate headquarters. This migration has resulted in a significant increase in the county's population and construction of schools, residential developments, and retail centers.

Loudoun's allegiance to the nation was tested during the War of 1812. While the British burned Washington, vital documents such as the Declaration of Independence and the Constitution were safely stowed away at Rokeby outside Leesburg. Loudoun's natural beauty and rural atmosphere inspired James Monroe to pen the Monroe Doctrine from his home at Oak Hill in 1823, and Franklin Delano Roosevelt was known to summer at Oatlands, the home of the Eustis family.

Preservation of history is evident in the towns and villages throughout Loudoun. Loudouners work fervently to preserve buildings, homes, and gardens of historical significance. Growing support among county supervisors has enabled Loudoun to safeguard several important sites. A newer trend throughout the county's older homes, estates, and farms is to convert them into bed-and-breakfasts and small conference centers. These reincarnations

Loudoun

dually maintain the scenery and create a new avenue of business for the county.

The Loudoun Museum, located in historic Leesburg, houses an impressive archive of the county's history and growth. It works in conjunction with other historical organizations. Several of these organizations grant awards to those who ardently restore private homes and fund educational programs within the school system. More than one dozen of the museum's programs are available throughout the school system. The Time Travelers program, sponsored by the state, is one example of the opportunities children have to vicariously travel the country. The program has found great success among Loudoun's younger generation. Walking tours and summer camps give adults and children alike a tactile and visual glimpse into Loudoun's past. Additionally, the county grants funding to

The Loudoun Museum houses an impressive archive of the county's history and growth. It works in conjunction with other historical organizations, several of which grant awards to those who ardently restore private homes and fund educational programs within the school system. Photo by David Galen.

Blending Tradition With Innovation

several of these programs, and many who choose to live in the county further the cause through generous donations and volunteerism.

The common thread among residents is the history bestowed to us by our ancestors. Loudouners continually underscore their dedication to the community and its heritage through many annual events. These events, interspersed throughout the year, draw as many locals as tourists. While Civil War reenactments memorialize fallen soldiers, August Court Days, sponsored by the Loudoun Restoration and Preservation Society, celebrates colonial Loudoun. This nonprofit group, along with others, works hard to champion our legacy. Visitors can interact with costumed street performers and colonial-day ladies and gentlemen. One can literally become a participant in an eighteenth-century wedding, public debate, or court trial.

Dedication to historical preservation is at its best when seen through local home and garden tours. One can step into a nineteenth-century mansion and feel the walls come alive with the events of the past. Visitors can stroll colonial herb gardens and capture the aroma of eighteenth-century life or visit the encampments of Civil War soldiers on the eve of battle. On a more cerebral level, one can witness a historical round table and gain insight into the issues of the time.

Singular to the county is the extraordinary generosity and commitment of residents in preserving Loudoun's oral history. Devotion to the county is indicative in the many descendants of original families as well as lifelong residents. Their wealth of knowledge and fond memories of life in the county are passed from generation to generation. They are tenacious in sustaining a link to the past through their homes, ideology, oral history, and celebration of the county's milestones.

Today, Loudoun is acutely aware of the importance of preserving the landscape. Local government, preservationists, historians, and residents work earnestly to find creative and cost-effective solutions to growth and conservation.

Large numbers of Quakers established themselves in Waterford and present-day Lincoln. The well-preserved mill stands as testament to the village of Waterford's early milling days. Photo by David Galen.

Loudoun

Blending Tradition With Innovation

Chapter Three

Economic Growth and Diversity

Geographical advantage is apparent in the economic success Loudoun sees today. The county's proximity to Washington Dulles International Airport introduces economic opportunities on an international, as well as national, level. Easy access to the airport, the addition of the Dulles Greenway—a privately funded toll road—a large, active business community, and close proximity to Washington, D.C., have contributed to the arrival of major corporations as well as a growing number of small and home-based businesses.

◤

The county's proximity to Washington Dulles International Airport introduces economic opportunities on an international, as well as a national, level. Photo by David Galen.

$\mathcal{M}$oreover, the Leesburg Executive Airport shelters many of the area's corporate jets and is capable of clearing travelers through U.S. customs as well. This modern facility was originally named Godfrey Field in honor of a past local resident and well-known entertainer, Arthur Godfrey.

Convenient accessibility to federal and local government offices solidifies Loudoun's reputation as a business center. Given the county's rate of growth, the transportation system is efficient. North and south connectors from Routes 7 and 28, as well as the addition of the Dulles Greenway, alleviate congestion for businesses and commuters in the area.

Loudoun's economic advantages are plentiful. Aside from the availability of land, those favoring a more rural setting are migrating to the county to establish businesses and residences, thereby bringing a substantial workforce with them. A favorable tax structure and the opportunity for campus development further enhance the allure of Loudoun's business base.

Currently, the rapid growth of the workforce and transportation have been two key issues the county has focused on. Large technology corporations employ an appreciable payroll. In our fast-paced society, these companies' needs must be addressed immediately and affirmatively. The Department of Economic Development has built a solid reputation through its efficient, professional, and swift response to the needs of area businesses. Local government is expeditious in providing personal service to its customers. Local officials are knowledgeable and supportive in providing all aspects of service to area businesses and residents.

The Department of Economic Development strives to ensure the economic strength and vitality of the whole community. There is a strong desire to be a national model for blending the traditional agricultural industry with the innovative technology industry. Local officials are intent on maintaining the small-town setting that draws residents, businesses, and tourists alike to the area. The symmetry between the high-tech industries and rural farmland is of vital importance to Loudoun's citizens. Diversity is a key ingredient to protecting the county's unique identity.

Loudoun continues to gain strength and recognition as a technology center in the eastern portion of the county, including the Town of Leesburg. The increasing number of small and home-based businesses complements the larger, more prominent corporations. Many of these businesses are off-shoots of the high-tech industry. Retail is also acquiring a large share of business in the county. The Leesburg Corner Premium Outlets has drawn shoppers within Loudoun County as well as those from Maryland and other northern Virginia counties.

Retail construction is introduced judiciously as well. The Dulles Town Center was on the developer's drawing board for 10 years before breaking ground. This measure ensures there will be adequate demand for such centers before development takes place. Dulles Town Center is Loudoun's first indoor mall encompassing over 1 million square feet and 140 stores. Nationally known retail stores

Blending Tradition With Innovation

are abundant in the eastern portion of the county, and the more specialized retailers are peppered evenly throughout the county.

As a substantial contributor to the nation's economy, Loudoun is gaining recognition as a national technology center. Corporations such as MCI WorldCom, America Online, and Orbital Sciences contribute to Loudoun's stature as a driving force on the information highway. The Virginia Center for Innovative Technology, near Dulles Airport, assists many of the technology companies in developing new technology and forming partnerships between corporations, local colleges, universities, and federal laboratories to create new services and products. Many of the area's institutions, such as George Washington University, Strayer University, Shenandoah University, George Mason University, Marymount University's Loudoun Center, and Northern Virginia Community College, allow companies to recruit students and utilize educational programs for their employees. Several of these universities and corporations share their facilities, including

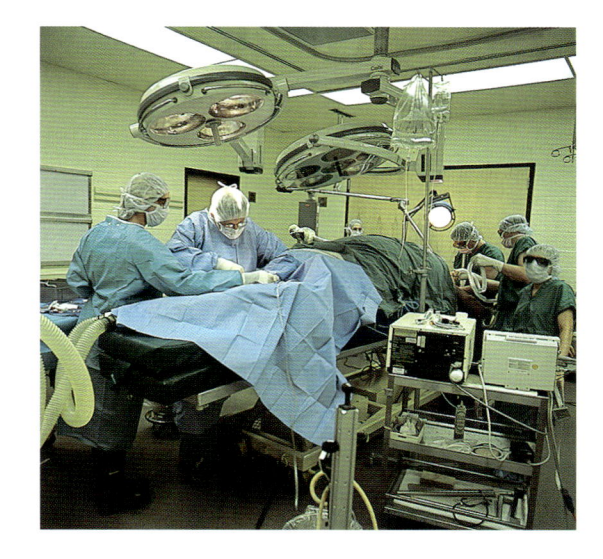

The fertile soil of the region is conducive to the production of wine. More than a dozen vineyards and wineries dot the countryside. Photo by David Galen.

Loudoun's equine heritage is apparent in the preeminent health care services available at the Marion duPont Scott Equine Center at Morven Park. Photo by David Galen.

The Virginia Center for Innovative Technology assists many of the technology companies in developing new technology and forming partnerships between corporations, local colleges, universities, and federal laboratories to create new services and products. Photo by David Galen.

laboratories and faculty. The county's impressive public school system and wide selection of higher institutions of learning appeal to a highly skilled workforce.

The focus on technology in the east harmonizes well with the productive agricultural industry in the western portion of Loudoun. Farming has been a mainstay in the county since its inception. The diversity of industries such as horses, cattle, llamas, and wine adds to the variety of interests present in Loudoun. The horse industry is a multimillion-dollar business for the county. Loudoun is renowned as a host to several international equestrian events annually. Over 33,000 Angus and Hereford cattle reside in the county.

A little-known and somewhat surprising trade is llama production. Today, there is at least one llama farm where visitors can lead llamas, laden with picnic baskets of culinary delights and replete with a local wine, to a babbling brook to enjoy a candlelight dinner. The fertile soil of the region is conducive to the production of wine. More than a dozen vineyards and six wineries dot the countryside. Several of these wines have been awarded international acclaim. Currently, there is a strong emphasis on preserving the rural aspects of the county. The county is working hard to ensure that

the developing east and rural west can coexist peacefully.

A key element to thwarting overdevelopment is detailed plans for land usage. Loudoun is unique regarding land development. Its efficiency in planning development is a cornerstone of the county's philosophy. Local officials are confident that technology will not eclipse their agricultural industry but rather will bolster it to new and unprecedented levels. The county has designated a rural task force to work cooperatively with local and state officials to ensure preservation of the unspoiled farmland. Loudoun anticipates it will be a demonstration model for research in the field of biotechnology and its relation to the agricultural environment.

The balance maintained between speculative properties and leasing of space is due to the desirable locale. The strong economy contributes to quickly leased buildings, matching the pace of new office construction. The construction of many of these new offices allows and plans for improved transportation in and around their facilities and offers an assortment of products which meet the needs of both large and small employers. Loudoun anticipates the immediate needs of commuters, businesses, and landowners with foresight and serious consideration of the end result before

Blending Tradition With Innovation

County government is responsive to the proliferation of businesses settling in Loudoun, yet remains committed to sustaining a high standard of living for its residents. Photo by David Galen.

America Online is one of many high-technology companies located in Loudoun County. Easy access to Washington Dulles International Airport and a favorable tax structure are two of many economic advantages for businesses settling in the county. Photo by Victoria Cooper for AOL.

31

Loudoun

The diversity of industries such as horses, cattle, llamas, and wine adds to the variety of interests present in Loudoun. Photo by David Galen.

Beaumeade is one of several industrial parks emerging in the county. Photo by David Galen.

building commences. The addition of North Gate at Dulles has enhanced the county's infrastructure. Rapid growth in the Dulles area has led to the incorporation of a Dulles, Virginia, zip code.

The trends toward telecommuting and working within one's residential area are becoming desirable as well. The challenge of balancing economic growth with conservation is first and foremost in the minds of economic developers, businesses, and government. Loudoun is keenly aware that not all growth is good, and overbuilding can be as ineffective as underdeveloping. County government is responsive to the proliferation of businesses settling in Loudoun, yet remains committed to sustaining a high standard of living for its residents.

Loudoun's affluence and population continue to grow steadily as well. The county projects growth will double in the next 10 years. As local businesses and corporations establish themselves in Loudoun, the constant demand for employees allows for a stable employment rate among Loudouners and increases the county's desirability. The U.S. Census Bureau recently reported Loudoun County to be the third-fastest growing county in the United States.

The blend of procommunity and probusiness principles manifests itself through Loudoun's success. Its strong infrastructure, along with the integration of self-contained communities such as Ashburn and Cascades, creates a cohesiveness often lacking in other communities.

The Loudoun County Chamber of Commerce, the second-largest Chamber in Virginia, is proactive as an advocate for the network of businesses in Loudoun. The Chamber, open to change,

Blending Tradition With Innovation

respectful of the past, and mindful of the future, is representative of the economic climate found in Loudoun. Its members embody the diversity, innovation, dedication, and fortitude exhibited by Loudouners throughout history. The mission of the Chamber states it will be the "voice of business," supporting new and existing businesses.

Despite its rapid growth, Loudoun's "main street" character is highly visible. Distinct to Loudoun as well is the acceptance of citizens and businesspeople who want to be actively involved. Volunteer and civic organizations are very prevalent. Seniority and pedigree make little or no difference in the influence and input one can wield in the county. With many communities becoming disconnected from their residents, a real, thriving business center is palpable in many of Loudoun's towns and villages. Shopkeepers and professionals welcome the consumer in a personal way that is all but lost in today's anonymous society. Businesspeople and residents bring to Loudoun a vast array of personal and cultural experiences. They contribute to the unique flavor of the county. Professionals and retailers unequivocally share their vocations and interests with their clients. Shopkeepers greeting customers on a first-name basis are common. This sentiment is what draws many to revisit and reside in Loudoun County.

In the years to come, Loudoun's landscape will undoubtedly change. The challenge for the county is to hold fast to its vision by embracing and balancing the county's beauty with its progress. Loudoun truly is a land of opportunity. It is a chance to grow as an individual, family, business, or community. Exclusivity has no place in Loudoun. A stroll down any of the main streets in Loudoun encapsulates its range of history, commerce, and promise, bringing Loudoun into the next century while cherishing its past. ◢

Residents and visitors can enjoy open farmers' markets in several locations throughout the county. Patrons can select fresh, locally grown fruits, vegetables, and flowers from May through November at these markets. Photo by David Galen.

Loudoun

Blending Tradition With Innovation

Chapter Four

A Thriving Downtown Center

Unique to the character of Loudoun are the thriving downtown business centers. These bustling centers offer everything from antiques to fine restaurants to professional offices. They complement the growing number of national retail stores arriving in the area.

The desire among Americans to return to a small-town way of life is prevalent among the residents who choose to settle in Loudoun. Many towns host events creating solidarity among their residents. Photo by David Galen.

The Dulles Town Center, located at the junction of Routes 7 and 28, contains more than 125 stores and restaurants with Sears, Lord & Taylor, Hechts, and JCPenney as its anchor stores. The mall, years in the making, has been a boost to the county's retail economy. Photo by David Galen.

The county has recently constructed the Dulles Town Center. This complex, located at the junction of Routes 7 and 28, contains more than 125 stores and restaurants, with Sears, Lord & Taylor, Hechts, and JCPenney as its anchor stores. The mall, years in the making, has been a boost to the county's retail economy. The Leesburg Corner Premium Outlets, off the Route 15 Bypass, continue to be a work in progress. Upon completion, this outlet center will contain more than 100 nationally known upscale outlet stores as well as a food court.

The contrast in style between the two shopping centers echoes the county's effort to balance progress with tradition. The Leesburg Corner Premium Outlets are mindful of the county's traditional architecture with colonial facades and beautifully landscaped courtyards and promenades. Dulles Town Center lends itself to the modern landscape emerging in this corridor of the county. It is a contemporary structure with a sleek, expansive atrium illuminated by a colorful skylight. It is enveloped by mature trees, preserved during construction, and well-planned landscaping.

Despite the introduction of larger retail centers on the fringes of the county, local officials are resolute in their commitment to preserving the main street atmosphere downtown. Officials appreciate the vigor these areas offer the community. Many towns continuously maintain productive and attractive centers, enticing business professionals, retailers, and residents. Many towns have numerous buildings on the National Registry of Historic Landmarks. The county has managed to continue the area's tradition of small-town life without impeding the positive flow of progress. The accessibility of modern conveniences complements the area's main street character.

Loudoun has earned a reputation as a mecca for antique dealers and collectors in many of these business centers. Dealers display their treasures in visually appealing storefronts and historic homes. Each shop offers an eclectic array of collectibles from colonial America through the present. The downtown area is home to many unique gift shops within the villages and towns throughout the county. Visitors can purchase hard-to-find items, locally crafted gifts, as well as mainstream pieces. Shopkeepers are happy to oblige a visitor's special request and enthusiastically assist shoppers with their inquiries.

Loudoun County is witnessing an emergence of fine restaurants throughout its centers. Many restaurants have earned reputations for attracting the finest chefs in the country. These restaurants invite diners to enjoy the sophisticated ambiance of French cuisine in a cosmopolitan setting or the down-home comfort of a Southern meal in a restored mill. The upsurge and success of these restaurants is more than palatable. Often, proprietors restore the architectural facades of their establishments. Several area restaurants have gone to great lengths and expense to refurbish older buildings, ensuring the vitality of downtown life and contributing to the value of real estate within these business centers.

The First Friday Gallery Walk is a lucrative event for retailers. The first Friday of every month, from February through December, shopkeepers in Leesburg leave their doors open late. Patrons can leisurely browse an art gallery, antiques store, gift shop, and even a comic book shop while enjoying refreshments and hors d'oeuvres courtesy of the proprietors. The after-hours atmosphere is unhurried and conducive not only to a favorable profit margin but also reminiscent of an earlier time, when patrons knew shopkeepers on a personal level. It is reassuring to witness a downtown center that continues to pulsate beyond the realm of nine to five.

The town of Middleburg has implemented a unique marketing strategy dubbed Middleburg Bucks. With the influx of national chain and discount stores in Loudoun, merchants in Middleburg have banded together to ensure the longevity and viability of their businesses. With more than 40 percent of the town's revenue derived from retail sales, meals, business licenses, and transitory occupancy taxes, the town's tourists are a prime marketing venue. With tourists furnishing a substantial portion of Middleburg's earnings, the program anticipates drawing an affluent consumer base. The bucks are certificates presented by participating retailers, with the assistance of concierges and local inns, as a stimulus for customers visiting Middleburg. The objective is to provide an appealing and effective public relations program, while attracting a recurrent and quality customer base. While many towns would appreciate voluminous crowds flocking to their centers, Middleburg prefers a relatively smaller, steadier following.

Loudoun professionals are equally comfortable conducting business in their downtown offices as well as in the local coffee shop. It is one of the keys to the success and appeal of the business district. Physicians, attorneys, dentists, insurance agents, and stockbrokers commingle with vendors throughout the main streets of the county. Furthermore, the county's commitment to helping existing businesses grow is vital to the endurance of the downtown area. The centralized location of county offices accommodates businesses from all corners of the region.

The desire among Americans to return to a small-town way of life is prevalent among the residents who choose to settle in Loudoun. Many towns host events creating solidarity among their residents. Events such as the holiday parades, First Night, and Fourth of July celebrations call for community members to gather in the downtown area to partake in the festivities proceeding through the towns and villages within the county. Further evoking the desire for the communities of the past is the revival of country stores throughout the county. Towns such as Airmont, Bluemont, and Philomont are finding a genuine need and want for the old-fashioned general store. The ambiance

The Leesburg Corner Premium Outlets, upon completion, will contain more than 100 nationally known upscale outlet stores as well as a food court. The center is mindful of the county's traditional architecture with colonial facades and beautifully landscaped courtyards and promenades. Photo by David Galen.

Events such as the holiday parades, First Night, and Fourth of July celebrations call for community members to gather in the downtown area to partake in the festivities proceeding through the towns and villages within the county. Photo by David Galen.

Loudoun County is witnessing an emergence of fine restaurants, many of which have earned reputations for attracting the country's finest chefs. Diners are invited to enjoy the sophisticated ambiance of French cuisine in a cosmopolitan setting or the down-home comfort of a Southern meal in a restored mill. Photo by David Galen.

found in these markets recalls an era when patrons shopped for staples and caught up on local news. These family-owned operations contribute to the cohesiveness of the community.

Despite the flurry of activity these centers experience, cars patiently yield to pedestrians, and a car horn is virtually unheard of, aside from the driver greeting a passerby. Those traveling on foot welcome one another, and holding open a door is commonplace. Drivers and pedestrians rarely pass hastily through town. Perhaps it is the sight of tourists meandering down brick sidewalks and professionals lunching on courthouse benches that subdue the tendency to race through the day.

Two other traits Loudoun exemplifies are the visual chronicle of time as one navigates downtown and the melange of architecture found in each town. Drive through any town in the county and one can see the evolution of each center. The former blacksmith's shop becomes a metal foundry. The former bank reinvents itself as a first-class restaurant. Historic homes cater to Internet companies, and the venerable courthouse is juxtaposed with the sleek government center.

Architecture plays a pivotal role in the perennial allure of the county's downtown centers. The mixture of design and form among the homes and buildings in each town is indicative of the county's early settlers and the era in which they were erected. The incorporation of the Washington and Old Dominion Railroad at the turn of the century introduced an abundance of Victorian architecture to the county as city dwellers flocked to Loudoun to escape the summer heat. The simplicity and practicality of the Quakers is clearly evident in the architecture found in towns like Waterford. The profusion of these homes and buildings throughout the downtown districts have become visual textbooks of the county's history and progress.

The residents' devotion to the county is clearly evident in many of these homes, often owned by original families and longtime residents, who graciously share their homes' lineage. The town of Leesburg is one of many towns consciously preserving and maintaining its downtown center's composition.

These locations invite residents and visitors to enjoy an ice cream on a main street bench or a book under the shade of a stately oak in the town square. Passing through the downtown district elicits a sense of belonging, which strengthens these centers. The residents and businesses are not mutually exclusive. These centers do not shut down after regular business hours or on weekends. They are equally viable areas of business as well as pleasure and intermingle quite effectively.

While many residences are within walking distance to these centers, ample parking is available for those who choose to drive. Parking garages are aesthetically appealing, generous in proportion, and neatly tucked behind the facades of older buildings. These town centers are well-insulated from the more modern portions of the county. The central core is truly the heart of each town. In spite of the tremendous activity in these centers, each town is well-maintained. Restaurants, hotels, stores, and

Blending Tradition With Innovation

The Town of Leesburg is one of the area's many towns consciously preserving and maintaining its downtown center's composition. Photo by David Galen.

Located in the downtown area, the Leesburg Restaurant is a popular breakfast and lunch spot for the local business community catching up on the latest news in town. Photo by David Galen.

public areas are tidy, orderly, and managed with warmth, friendliness, and efficiency. It is one of the many reasons tourists visit each year and residents come to live.

The citizens' reverence for their centers is also seen in the heritage days celebrated throughout Loudoun's towns and villages. These annual events draw the community closer and commemorate the importance of a vital business district and its contributors. With the commitment of local officials and the dedication of business owners and residents, the county's downtown areas will continue to thrive. The addition of larger retail centers enhances the appeal of the downtown area and attracts a larger customer base.

Charm, beauty, and individuality radiate from each town, making Loudoun special. Loudouners never lose sight of their vision for the county and continually strive to improve the standard of living for all who come to the county. The intimate mood is evident to residents, professionals, and visitors alike. The humanity and vitality in these areas exemplify Loudoun.

Blending Tradition With Innovation

Not to be missed in this quaint Waterford Village, The Pink House serves as a bed-and-breakfast. Photo by David Galen.

Loudoun has earned a reputation as a mecca for antique dealers and collectors. Dealers display their treasures in visually appealing storefronts and historic homes. Photo by David Galen.

Loudoun

Blending Tradition With Innovation

Chapter Five

Cultural Enrichment Abounds

Cultural and family-oriented activities are plentiful in Loudoun County. The area offers a richly talented and eclectic array of performers. From the Bluemont Concert Series featuring jazz, classical, and bluegrass music to the Loudoun Ballet Company performing the classics, there is something to please every cultural palate.

Loudoun County offers a richly talented and eclectic array of performers. From the Loudoun Symphony to the Loudoun Ballet Company, there is something to please every cultural palate. Photo by David Galen.

Loudoun

Morven Park's equine association retains one of the largest personal collections of horse-drawn vehicles in its carriage museum. In keeping with its hunt tradition, the park also hosts the Virginia Foxhound Club Hound Show, Draft Horse and Mule Day, and the spring and fall horse trials. Photo by David Galen.

The Loudoun Tourism Council in Leesburg, established in 1995, works hard to promote Loudoun County and its incorporated towns. The county has been featured in several national magazines such as *Southern Living* and *Traditional Home* and, in 1998, welcomed more than 300,000 visitors to its historic destinations and special events. Tourism generates more than $260 million for the county and is continuing to gain momentum through the efforts of the Tourism Council and the county's exposure on the Internet. The county consistently observes an increase in tourists year-round, including international visitors. Many of the long-established events endure and continue to draw visitors annually.

Loudoun boasts several fine vineyards producing impressive wines. Vineyards like Tarara Winery welcome visitors to tour their facilities. Many offer events the entire family can enjoy, such as kite flying contests, holiday parties, and private affairs. The area is also carving a niche in microbrewery production. The Old Dominion Beer Fest includes more than a dozen Virginia draft breweries and provides food, entertainment, and even a Brewer's Olympics.

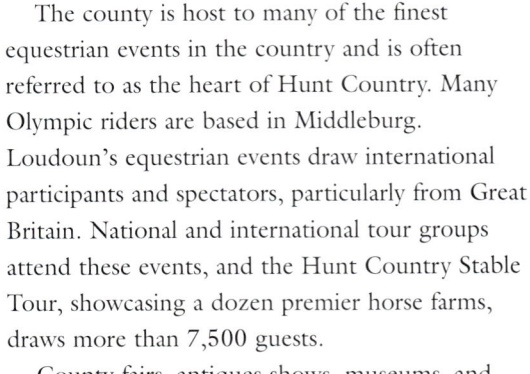

The county is host to many of the finest equestrian events in the country and is often referred to as the heart of Hunt Country. Many Olympic riders are based in Middleburg. Loudoun's equestrian events draw international participants and spectators, particularly from Great Britain. National and international tour groups attend these events, and the Hunt Country Stable Tour, showcasing a dozen premier horse farms, draws more than 7,500 guests.

County fairs, antiques shows, museums, and sporting events provide wholesome fun for all generations. The Tourism Council cites fairs and festivals as its most frequently inquired about events. Fairs such as Lucketts, Bluemont, and the Loudoun 4-H produce a tremendous turnout.

These fairs are bigger and better each year and prove the county's dedication to tradition and community life. Book fairs also draw many from near and far, and the proceeds often support one of many local charities. Many of the area's antiques shows bring out avid collectors and dealers from as far as California. Several items have auctioned at phenomenal prices.

Loudoun offers myriad recreation facilities and parks. A few of the more prominent parks, including the Washington and Old Dominion Trail, command arresting views. With over a dozen golf courses, the county is gaining prominence as a premier golf center. Two prominent courses are located in Leesburg. Raspberry Falls Golf and Hunt Club is a new establishment with a course designed by Gary Player. Lansdowne Conference Center features a course designed by Robert Trent Jones Jr. and hosts the Bobby Mitchell Hall of Fame Golf Classic, attracting more than 40 Hall of Fame players. German tourists, in particular, have expressed interest in the golf facilities offered within the county.

The county's park system is an integral part of the quality of life in Loudoun. With more than 16 parks in the county's jurisdiction, there is a distinctive flavor within each park. Notable among these parks is the Washington and Old Dominion Railroad Regional Park and Trail. This expansive trail wends its way through the bucolic countryside

Blending Tradition With Innovation

of Loudoun. The 45-mile-long path extends from Purcellville to Arlington. This popular trail is traversed by runners, walkers, and cyclists, while equestrian riders use the parallel gravel trail. It is one of the oldest rails to trails.

Many Loudoun County parks provide playgrounds, swimming pools, golf courses, tennis and basketball courts, and playing fields. These parks are often equipped with picnic areas, and several offer fishing and boating facilities. A common thread among several parks is the observation of the county's history. Ball's Bluff Regional Park is the most renowned, with its memorial to fallen Civil War soldiers. Temple Hill Farm Regional Park pays homage to the agricultural heritage and influence of the area through its recreation of a working farm. The Loudoun Heritage Farm Museum, constructed at Claude Moore Park, features artifacts and farm equipment from the eighteenth- and nineteenth centuries. Loudoun also offers its residents and guests an insightful guide to farm life through its annual Loudoun Farms Tour held in the spring and fall.

Visitors can take a self-guided tour of the area's agricultural farms and delight in the flora and fauna. Patowmack Farm, a certified organic producer, embodies the agricultural importance of the county. Whites' Ferry provides a stunning view of the Potomac as it ferries passengers, cars, and bikes from Leesburg to Poolesville, Maryland. Access to the Maryland side invites passengers to picnic areas and canoe and boat rentals along the C & O Canal. The ferry is considered to be the oldest running diesel ferry in the country and is utilized by commuters to Maryland and D.C. suburbs.

Naturalists will find a multitude of parks and facilities catering to their appreciation of nature. Leesburg's Red Rocks Wilderness Overlook Regional Park is a preserved aviary sanctuary. Winding through the 67-acre park are wooded

With over a dozen courses, Loudoun County is recognized as a premier golf center. Raspberry Falls Golf and Hunt Club is a new establishment with a course designed by Gary Player. Photo by David Galen.

45

The Potomac Celtic Festival celebrates the cultures of Ireland, Scotland, Wales, and the other Celtic nations. The two-day festival includes Highland athletics, wine and malt whiskey tastings, historical reenactments, Celtic import vendors, food, music, dance, and storytelling. Photo by David Galen.

trails leading to a scenic overlook of the Potomac River. Nature enthusiasts can make their way to the Smithsonian Institution's Naturalist Center. This center, located in Leesburg, is part of the National Museum of Natural History and offers hands-on study of natural artifacts.

Loudoun has a strong foothold within the cultural arts community. The county boasts several musical organizations, such as American Children of SCORE, Loudoun Community Band, Loudoun Concert Orchestra, Loudoun Symphony, and the Neale Concert Series with its local classical musicians. Residents are undoubtedly familiar with the Bluemont Concert Series presented each June through August. For a nominal fee, visitors can enjoy an expansive range of performances covering everything from classical and jazz to calypso and swing. Attendees are encouraged to bring a picnic supper and blanket to spread out on the courthouse lawn in Leesburg. The Waterford Concert Series offers world-renowned performances, including the U.S. Navy Band and regional finalists from the Metropolitan Opera.

Perhaps it is the rural serenity that makes Loudoun so conducive to the arts. Loudoun offers a plethora of organizations for all levels of ability and interest. The budding artist can attend Arts in a Nutshell in Purcellville. Here, small children can hone their skills through any number of courses. The Loudoun Sketch Club promotes exhibits and shows throughout the calendar year. In keeping with the county's openness and diversity, The Transcendental Arts Council promotes the innovation of the artist through its alliance of artisans from various backgrounds. The Loudoun Ballet Company is a federally funded, nonprofit organization performing traditional and contemporary dances. It is open to adults and children and has performed in Europe and New York. Its fine performances of *Peter and the Wolf* and *The Nutcracker* are widely acclaimed throughout the county. In the tradition of the county's Southern roots, the Bluemont Country Dances draw many regulars to dance and socialize.

While arts in Loudoun are generously supported by various patrons and residents, the Loudoun Arts Council enhances the cultural community through its advocation, assistance, and promotion of the county's artists and programs. The county's appreciation of art is also evident in the many art shows held annually. Craft shows are plentiful as well, and artisans exhibit a wide range of talent.

Both Morven Park and Oatlands Plantation play host to numerous annual events. Both hold court over point-to-point and steeplechase races, as well as holiday house tours and horse shows. Oatlands holds antiques fairs in the spring and fall as well as an herb fair, sheepdog trials, Loudoun County Day, and the Middleburg Classic Horse Show. Morven Park's equine association is solid and well-known. It retains one of the largest personal collections of horse-drawn vehicles in its

Blending Tradition With Innovation

carriage museum, and its grounds include a mansion with priceless antiques and artifacts collected by Westmoreland Davis and his wife throughout their world travels. In keeping with its hunt tradition, the park also hosts the Virginia Foxhound Club Hound Show, Draft Horse and Mule Day, and a Sporting Art Exhibit and Sale, as well as the spring and fall horse trials. One can also peruse more than 12,000 books on horse and field sports dating back to the sixteenth century at the National Sporting Library.

Spring, summer, and fall in Loudoun give way to an abundance and variety of festivals. The Leesburg Flower and Garden Festival is a welcome sign that spring has arrived, and attendance and participation continue to grow each year. Horticulturalists can enjoy a second flower festival at Field of Flowers and many strawberry festivals each summer. Middleburg presents one of the area's eminent garden tours, drawing more than 2,500 tourists.

Tradition is a mainstay in the county and is manifested in events such as the Potomac Celtic Festival, which celebrates the cultures of Ireland, Scotland, Wales, and the other Celtic nations. The two-day festival includes Highland athletics, wine and malt whiskey tastings, historical reenactments, Celtic import vendors, food, music, dance, and storytelling.

True to its German heritage, Lovettsville holds its own Oktoberfest. Taste of the Towns provides visitors with a culinary banquet presented by local restaurants. The sampling illustrates the diversity in the county's cuisine. One can feast on the food of the Pacific Rim, a French province, northern Italy, and China along with dishes native to the area.

For transportation lovers, Washington Dulles International Airport contributes to the entertainment found within the county. One can observe an air show, visit the aviation museum, or cheer on competitors in a plane pull. America's love affair with the car continues at the Classic Car Show. Car enthusiasts display their automotive jewels ranging from Model As to 1960s Mustangs.

Certainly, the county's roles in the Revolutionary and Civil Wars are demonstrated in reenactments, August Court Days, and the Fife and Drum Corps. Over 30 fife and drum corps representing more than nine states make their way through historic downtown Leesburg annually. European interest in the Civil War attracts many

White's Ferry provides a stunning view of the Potomac as it ferries passengers, cars, and bikes from Leesburg to Poolesville, Maryland. The ferry is considered to be the oldest running diesel ferry in the country and is utilized by commuters to Maryland and D.C. suburbs. Photo by David Galen.

Loudoun

The Bluemont Concert Series, presented each June through August, provides music lovers with an expansive range of performances covering everything from classical and jazz to calypso and swing. Photo by David Galen.

America's love affair with the car continues at the Classic Car Show. Car enthusiasts display their automotive jewels ranging from Model As to 1960s Mustangs. Photo by David Galen.

international visitors to enjoy the area's historic roundtables. Followers of the occult can join one of many ghost tours, particularly around Halloween. The area is ripe with alleged hauntings, and folklore heightens the mystery of these sites.

Each town exudes a unique distinction and charm, elevating Loudoun's allure. Night life in the eastern part of the county, access to Washington, D.C., and limitless accommodations and travel complement the rural backdrop in the western portion of Loudoun. One can retreat to a gentrified setting, yet remain accessible to more cosmopolitan D.C. The unparalleled quality of Loudoun's culture and beauty induces many travel writers to frequent the area. The cultural and sporting communities personify Loudoun's warmth, hospitality, tradition, diversity, and innovation, making it an idyllic destination for visitors and the ultimate residence for politicians, celebrities, farmers, horse breeders, and families alike.

The Washington and Old Dominion Trail wends its way through the bucolic countryside of Loudoun. The 45-mile-long path, which extends from Purcellville to Arlington, is traversed by runners, walkers, cyclists, and equestrian riders who use the parallel gravel trail. Photo by David Galen.

Loudoun

Blending Tradition With Innovation

Chapter Six

Generosity of Spirit

Loudouners ardently support community efforts to enhance the quality of life for their neighbors. This quality of life can, in part, be attributed to the residents who generously and tirelessly volunteer their time, resources, and talents to aiding causes such as the local women's shelter, soup kitchen, and animal shelter. They are attuned to the needs of all residents, regardless of race, creed, age, or ability. Residents provide informational, educational, financial, and training support to a legion of programs benefiting the community.

◤

A large share of Loudoun's appeal lies in its affinity for livestock and pets. With its deep agricultural history, Loudoun's 4-H program continues to thrive. Photo by David Galen.

Programs and opportunities for senior citizens are prevalent in Loudoun County. Loudoun's Agency on Aging is at the core of many senior programs, providing assistance and information to senior citizens and their families. Photo by David Galen.

The number of attendees to the county's fairs and festivals gives credence to their desire to embrace and partake in the spirit of community and generosity. Kids Day at Ida Lee Park celebrates the family and supports local organizations such as Interfaith Relief. Participants can enjoy games, rides, music, food, and entertainment for a nonperishable or monetary donation to Interfaith.

Interfaith Relief provides free emergency food to anyone in need. The program is bolstered by more than a dozen interdominational county churches. An extension of Interfaith Relief is Daily Bread, offering a free nightly meal to those in need. The Interfaith/Daily Bread organization has a tremendous core of volunteers who stock shelves and collect and distribute food throughout the year. Many of the area schools conduct food drives during the school year, enabling Interfaith shelves to remain well-stocked.

Programs and opportunities for senior citizens are prevalent in the county. Loudoun's Agency on Aging is at the core of many senior programs. They provide assistance and information to senior citizens and their families.

Elder Choices connects seniors with the community services they need, including legal services and transportation. Buses transport seniors to shopping and downtown centers throughout the county. Those physically or mentally confined to home may receive a meal as well as assistance preparing food.

Title V is a program presenting work opportunities to people over 55, meeting income eligibility requirements. The Mature Worker program enables eligible seniors to receive individual job placement and training assistance.

The Retired and Senior Volunteer Program encourages senior citizens to share their talents and abilities through volunteer service. Volunteers work at various sites throughout Loudoun County, including thrift shops, CAFEs, and on special projects such as the Tax Preparation Assistance Program and the Virginia Insurance Counseling and Advocacy Project.

Senior CAFEs provide meals to seniors five days per week. Activities such as shopping, movies, and exercise are also offered to seniors. Transportation is provided and available to the handicapped. The Adult Day Care/Respite Center provides therapeutic activities for the chronically disabled and alleviates a measure of responsibility from family members. Assisted living facilities such as Morningside and

Sunrise are designed to be warm, personal atmospheres. They are extremely well-maintained and efficiently run.

Community Connections is a case management and day activity program for brain-injured adults within Loudoun County. The program holds bimonthly support groups for survivors and caregivers in conjunction with the Northern Virginia Brain Injury Association. Loudoun Therapeutic Riding Foundation, Inc. is a therapeutic horseback riding program for disabled youth and adults. The program relies on volunteers to serve as leaders for mounts and sidewalkers for students.

Programs for the mentally challenged are plentiful in the county. The Department of Mental Health and Mental Retardation provides foster care and oversees group homes for mentally retarded adults. Additionally, the department advocates equal opportunities in community life by assisting mentally handicapped individuals and their families in fulfilling their potential. It also provides financial support for respite care, adaptive equipment, and other supplies associated with home care.

Additionally, the department offers education programs including physical and speech therapy, as well as testing for handicapped infants and toddlers. Loudoun Association of Retarded Citizens operates several successful programs. Special Olympics, Teen Vocational, Summer Work, and Special Friends programs are available as well as advocacy, parent support, and camp experiences. Echo, Inc.(Every Citizen Has Opportunities) has implemented a work environment to evaluate, train, and place the retarded, mentally ill, and physically handicapped in various employment capacities.

Very Special Arts-Loudoun County Theatre Troupe is composed of mentally and physically disabled actors and proudly represented the state of Virginia with its recent performance of *Daniel Boone in the Old Dominion* in Los Angeles at the International Special Arts Festival. The trip was funded by Loudoun citizens, businesses, churches, civic organizations, board of supervisors, and fundraising proceeds. The success of the program hinges on the staunch support of volunteers and contributors within the community.

Blue Ridge Speech and Hearing Center offers screening, evaluation, and therapy for hearing, speech, and language. NOVA West-Self Help for the Hard of Hearing is an informational and support group for those confronting hearing loss.

Loudoun Abused Women's Shelter provides temporary emergency shelter for abused women and their children. The shelter offers 24-hour crisis

The Loudoun County Department of Parks and Recreation operates 10 community centers. Photo by David Galen.

In 1998, Loudouners overwhelmingly voted to renovate the Loudoun Animal Shelter located in Waterford. The shelter has an Adopt A Pet program as well as a dedicated group of volunteers and supporters. Photo by David Galen.

Through the Loudoun County Department of Parks and Recreation, young and old alike are encouraged to participate in a wide variety of programs ranging from educational courses to sporting events. Photo by David Galen.

intervention, transportation, weekly support groups, children's programs, and court advocacy. The Resourceful Woman is a secondhand store offering clothing, toys, books, and housewares to the general public. Their efforts and proceeds support the Women's Shelter. The Women's Resource Center supplies women with educational workshops, support groups, a reference library pertaining to women's issues, professional development programs, and job listings.

Homelessness is addressed by many in the community. Programs such as Christmas in April are widely recognized and well-received by county residents. Each Christmas in April house is the work of many dedicated volunteers and suppliers, pledging their time and materials toward the construction of homes for lower-income families. The Office of Housing Services supports Christmas in April and other affordable housing initiatives for first-time, low-income home buyers. The Transitional Housing Shelter provides housing for a maximum of 44 homeless persons. Counseling, budget training, and basic living skills are also offered. Good Shepherd Alliance assists individuals in crisis situations through provisions in shelter, food, clothing, financial counseling, and other referral services.

Family programs like the Virginia Cooperative Extension are designed to improve the quality of life for families through instruction in financial planning, nutrition, and parenting. Young Parents Network is offered through the Department of Social Services and offers guidance in prenatal and postnatal care, childbirth, parenting, and child care.

Beyond the basic necessities met by these organizations, Loudoun offers many informational and referral services catering to mental and physical health, including substance abuse, teen pregnancy, and child abuse. Loudoun Communities That Care is a program intent on reducing adolescent behavioral problems.

Community centers and park services provide abundant after school and child care programs throughout the county. The Loudoun County Department of Parks, Recreation, and Community Services operates 10 community centers. All centers encourage young and old alike to participate in a wide variety of programs ranging from educational courses to sporting events and field trips.

Employment and training programs are available in Loudoun as well. The Department of Social Services offers remedial education, employment, and training programs, as well as Mentoring for Success, matching business mentors with adults seeking to enter or reenter the workforce. With the guidance of mentors, definitive objectives and goals can be achieved during the six-month commitment. Summer Job Match offers young people summer employment opportunities.

Spiritual fulfillment plays an integral part in maintaining a strong community. Loudoun offers a spiritual refuge for all denominations. Many of these denominations fully encourage and support community awareness and involvement. Many participate in holiday coalitions, food drives, clothing, and infant supply collections for families in need, as well as transportation of senior citizens to services, doctors' appointments, and shopping. The spiritual fulfillment and generosity of area churches and religious organizations are vital to the community.

Aiding local families and individuals in need is possible through organizations such as LINK, Inc. This network of more than a dozen churches assists Sterling and Herndon residents in crisis. Shops such as Blossom and Bloom, The Resourceful Woman, and Good Shepherd Clothes House offer low-cost clothing, furniture, and household goods to anyone in need. All items are generously donated by local residents.

Loudoun's fire and rescue volunteers number more than 1,000 and staff 20 stations. These citizens volunteer their time to work 12-hour shifts, including weekends, while holding down full-time jobs. They undergo extensive training with a minimum of 140 course hours. Their dedication to their community and its members is unparalleled.

Loudoun has been the recipient of gifts from philanthropic benefactors, including Paul Mellon and Irwin Wayne Uran, both of whom were deeply affected by the warmth and natural beauty of the area. Their gifts are a testament to the unsurpassed bounty of Loudoun. Over the years, Mr. Mellon bequeathed gifts to Middleburg's community center, founded the National Sporting Library, funded the construction of the Virginia Tech Center, and was a longtime benefactor to Hill School. In keeping with the county's long-standing love of horses, he donated a full-size bronze horse sculpture to the Virginia Historical Society in commemoration of the scores of horses maimed or killed during the Civil War. Although a reclusive man, Mr. Uran felt a kinship with Loudouners and has contributed unselfishly to many Loudoun organizations. In 1997, Mr. Uran left the Town of Leesburg $1 million to help children, particularly troubled youths. In 1998, a Leesburg synagogue received a gift of $2 million from him. Mr. Uran's generous gifts are a tribute to this unique community.

A large share of Loudoun's appeal lies in its affinity for livestock and pets. With its deep agricultural history, Loudoun's 4-H program continues to thrive. The program allows young members to develop leadership skills, acquire new talents, and nurture friendships. There are several groups within the organization, and turnout is strong at local competitions. In 1998, Loudouners overwhelmingly voted to renovate the Loudoun Animal Shelter located in Waterford. The shelter has an Adopt A Pet program as well as a dedicated group of volunteers and supporters.

Loudoun offers a plethora of services and organizations to residents. All of Loudoun's

Loudoun's fire and rescue volunteers number more than 1,000 and staff 20 stations. These citizens volunteer their time to work 12-hour shifts, including weekends, while holding down full-time jobs. Photo by David Galen.

Loudoun

An extension of Interfaith Relief, Daily Bread offers a free nightly meal to those in need. The Interfaith/ Daily Bread organization has a tremendous core of volunteers who stock shelves and collect and distribute food throughout the year. Photo by David Galen.

organizations are worthwhile, and its volunteers and supporters are recognized for their unwavering allegiance to sustaining and improving these programs. A drive through any neighborhood reinforces this sense of community. Neighbors watch over children, share gardening tools, and hold block parties. Families prepare meals and tend to errands for those facing a crisis. In an era of transience, neighbors take the time to know one another. The spirit of generosity prevails in Loudoun as it holds steadfast to tradition, while embracing change. ◢

Blending Tradition With Innovation

Loudoun Therapeutic Riding Foundation, a therapeutic horseback riding program for disabled youth and adults, relies on volunteers to serve as leaders for mounts and sidewalkers for students. Photo by Gail A. Williams.

Loudoun

Blending Tradition With Innovation

Chapter Seven

Higher Standards of Learning

Loudoun's commitment to higher standards of learning and its wide range of educational options draw many families to the county. Loudoun is home to more than a dozen private schools, universities, and colleges, as well as numerous public elementary, middle, and high schools that offer progressive and rigorous curriculums. Additionally, the county has several vocational and technical schools.

Programs for gifted students are available at all grade levels in every school. Students meeting specific requirements may attend Governor's Magnet School programs in science and technology, as well as the visual and performing arts. Photo by Bill Denison.

Loudoun

Northern Virginia Community College provides horticulture programs in keeping with the county's agricultural roots. Photo by David Galen.

Monroe Technology Center has a nationally recognized automotive technology facility. The program offers student internships with local automobile dealers. Photo by David Galen.

As the 11th largest public school system in Virginia, Loudoun County's educational programs rank among the best in the state. The county's steady stream of young families has accelerated the construction of many new schools.

Loudoun County is among the most rapidly growing school systems in the nation and the fastest growing in Virginia. More than 20 additional schools will have commenced or completed construction by the year 2005. These new facilities provide abundant learning opportunities for students and exciting and challenging career opportunities for teachers. The county currently has more than 45 schools with average class sizes at 20 per kindergarten class with a teacher and teacher's assistant, 22 for grades first through third, 25 for grades fourth and fifth, and 21.6 and 26.6 at the middle and high school levels respectively.

Achievement tests indicate the county continues to rank among the top 10 out of 130 school systems in the state. SAT scores for Loudoun's college-bound high school seniors consistently surpass those for the state and nation. The dropout rate for grades 7 through 12 is among the lowest in Virginia and the United States. Seventy-three percent of Loudoun high school students taking advanced placement tests achieve high scores of three or better, thereby becoming eligible for college credit. Advanced placement courses range from history, calculus, and English to science and the foreign languages. Ninety-eight percent of Loudoun's high school seniors graduate, with 87 percent continuing formal education and 80 percent entering college.

Programs for gifted students are available at all grade levels in every school. Students meeting specific requirements may attend Governor's Magnet School programs in science and technology, as well as the visual and performing arts. Comprehensive special education services are provided to Loudoun youngsters with disabilities. The county's public schools have received statewide recognition for their model programs to include disabled students in the regular classroom environment.

Educational programs are not limited to the young. Adult education for residents 18 and older is available through an Adult Basic Education program, including English as a second language, reading, writing, mathematics, and communications. Head Start offers a preschool program for economically disadvantaged families at several centrally located elementary schools.

Despite the challenge of growth, need for additional schools, and funding, Loudoun County is maintaining the quality of its school system. Support among parents and the public, as well as consistent funding, have played a pivotal role in the school system's success. During the past decade, bond referendums for school construction have won widening margins of voter support across the county. With a referendum each year, Loudouners clearly understand the importance of quality public education for the community.

Loudoun continues its cost-effective approach to school construction without compromising the quality of newly built schools. In line with community expectations, the school system continues to build state-of-the-art, technologically advanced facilities. Per-square-foot construction costs for Loudoun's new elementary and middle schools have consistently been below state averages. Growth within the school system also presents a healthy challenge, as the recruitment effort for more than 400 new teachers annually has become a year-round program. Nationwide recruitment, competitive pay for teachers, and challenging staff development programs help Loudoun employ highly qualified personnel.

Ninety-four percent of Loudoun County Public School employees are school-based to serve students, and according to the *D.C. Metro Area Board of Education Guide*, Loudoun boasts the highest percentage of school-based personnel in the region.

The area's technological focus is apparent in the county's public schools. Students at all grade levels have access to the latest technological learning tools. As early as kindergarten, students are taught to use the computer and begin to learn its capabilities as an aid to classroom instruction. The school system pioneered and completed a comprehensive technology implementation plan in the spring of 1999.

This plan equips each classroom with a minimum of four state-of-the-art computers. Each middle school maintains three computer laboratories in addition to technology education labs. Each high school is appointed with six networked computer laboratories. Every Loudoun public school library and public school classroom provides students and teachers with controlled access to telecommunications services and the global information resources of the Internet via the school system's computer network. High schools and the Monroe Technology Center are equipped with satellite dishes for remote learning and teleconferencing.

Computer training for teachers is a unique component of instructional technology in the classroom. Teachers are required to complete a minimum of seven days of training, featuring classes at the school system's staff training center and additional collaborative work in their schools with technical resource teachers and computer lab aides.

Monroe Technology Center has a nationally recognized automotive technology facility. The center also offers high school students advanced

Loudoun County's educational programs rank among the best in the state. The county's steady stream of young families has accelerated the construction of many new schools. Photo by David Galen.

Loudoun County is among the most rapidly growing school systems in the nation and the fastest growing in Virginia. Photo by David Galen.

The Paxton Development Center is one of many child care alternatives offered to working parents. Paxton Development Center, located in Leesburg, is situated on a farm comprised of many animals. Photo by David Galen.

training in 17 specialized vocational/technical fields. General Motors selected Monroe as the nation's premier school to pilot the GM-YES Program. The program offers student internships with local automobile dealers. The Practical Nursing School at Monroe Technology Center is a mutually beneficial partnership with Loudoun Hospital, established over 20 years ago. Classroom training at Monroe is reinforced with clinical experience at the hospital.

With the arrival of new businesses and corporations, the school system has expanded its active school-business partnership program to include such global enterprises as AOL, Telos, Orbital Sciences, Tellabs, and Xerox. Their support for public education and expertise are essential to Loudoun's commitment to first-class school programs and services.

These companies value and support the importance of education in Loudoun. It is an enticing benefit for attracting and retaining employees. Job For A Day is a program offered through the myriad business partnerships fostered within Loudoun schools. High school juniors select an area of interest, and the partnership council locates businesses to employ students for a day. Funding is consistently supported by this segment of the community.

AOL, Telos, and Orbital Sciences have partnerships with Loudoun schools and involvement within the classroom. AOL assisted one area school with the installation of its computers and collaborated with another school to create an on-line calendar for each grade level. Blending traditional instruction with new technology tools has become a standard in Loudoun's school system. AOL assists teachers in developing web sites at individual schools and works in coalition with technology resource teachers. All school employees work together to incorporate a balance between formal education and technology.

Parents continue to be proactive in Loudoun schools. Loudoun Education Alliance of Parents (LEAP) is a countywide parent group meeting monthly. Comprised of delegates from every school parent group, LEAP members share ideas and maintain an open line of communication with Loudoun's education superintendent. This support group acts as a liaison between the school board and individual schools. Parents Love A Neighborhood School (PLANS) represents parents in western Loudoun. Its focus is on anticipating future growth, funding, and educational issues. While this part of the county is developing at a slower pace, PLANS is indicative of the forward-thinking characteristic of Loudoun residents.

The Loudoun Education Foundation (LEF) is a nonprofit group raising funds to enhance school programs. Scholarships to summer school, particularly for needy elementary age children and financial aid for college students, are awarded by the foundation. The annual Excellence in Education Banquet, cosponsored by the foundation and school system, recognizes outstanding high school seniors maintaining an A average. The banquet also honors the students' favorite teachers, their parents, and an outstanding principal for the year. The foundation funds grants to teachers who develop innovative and creative learning projects for the classroom.

Tradition and innovation, along with a supportive community, in the face of rapid growth define the character of the Loudoun school system. True to the county's desire to blend the old with the new, Loudoun schools are deeply committed to instilling the traditional aspects of education, such as music and the arts, in their students.

Loudoun's public schools, in conjunction with George Washington University's Virginia campus and Shenandoah University, instituted The Jazz Lab and Jam Session in 1996. The program encourages mentors and recognizes young, talented musicians in Loudoun. The ingenious program presents diverse jazz styles through a host of ensembles.

The George Washington University Faculty Jazz Quintet and the Shenandoah Conservatory Faculty Jazz Septet are representative of Loudoun's exceptional music programs. The county's young, gifted musicians are featured in the Loudoun All-County High School Jazz Band. The public can enjoy these presentations in several venues, including Lansdowne and Basin Street Jazz Club, as well as a Jazz Lab. The Jazz Lab workshop features music faculty from George Washington and Shenandoah, as well as five public high school jazz ensembles. Students gain insight from professional jazz musicians and music professors into music, instruments, composers, and the commitment needed to succeed.

George Washington University's Virginia campus serves an international technology and management community. It is noted for its executive and accelerated graduate programs. It is gaining prominence as a leading researcher in engineering, information technology, business, human resource development, and higher education.

Shenandoah University has more than 60 programs of study at the undergraduate and graduate levels. Shenandoah's Loudoun Center offers graduate degrees for teachers and school administrators, as well as those pursuing careers in education.

Strayer University offers an array of computer and business courses. Master's, bachelor's and associate's degrees can be obtained at its Ashburn campus.

Northern Virginia Community College (NOVA) maintains five campuses and is the state's largest institution of higher learning. In keeping with the county's agricultural roots, the Loudoun campus, located in Sterling, provides horticulture and veterinary technology programs. Courses in computers, liberal arts, science, business, and fine arts are also available.

George Mason University maintains a professional location at the Center for Innovative Technology. Its training facilities are utilized by the Executive M.B.A. degree program, Center of Professional Development Executive programs, and the Professional Center.

Marymount University's Sterling campus is an extension of the main campus in Arlington. Undergraduate and graduate liberal arts programs are available.

Education remains the cornerstone of the Loudoun community. Parents, teachers, administrators, and businesses have worked diligently to set and preserve a standard of excellence in Loudoun schools. The Loudoun school system seamlessly incorporates today's technology with yesterday's conventional methods of education, thus ensuring a promising future for Loudoun's children.

Achievement tests indicate that Loudoun County continues to rank among the top 10 out of 130 school systems in the state. SAT scores for Loudoun's college-bound high school seniors consistently surpass those for the state and nation. Photo by David Galen.

Loudoun

Blending Tradition With Innovation

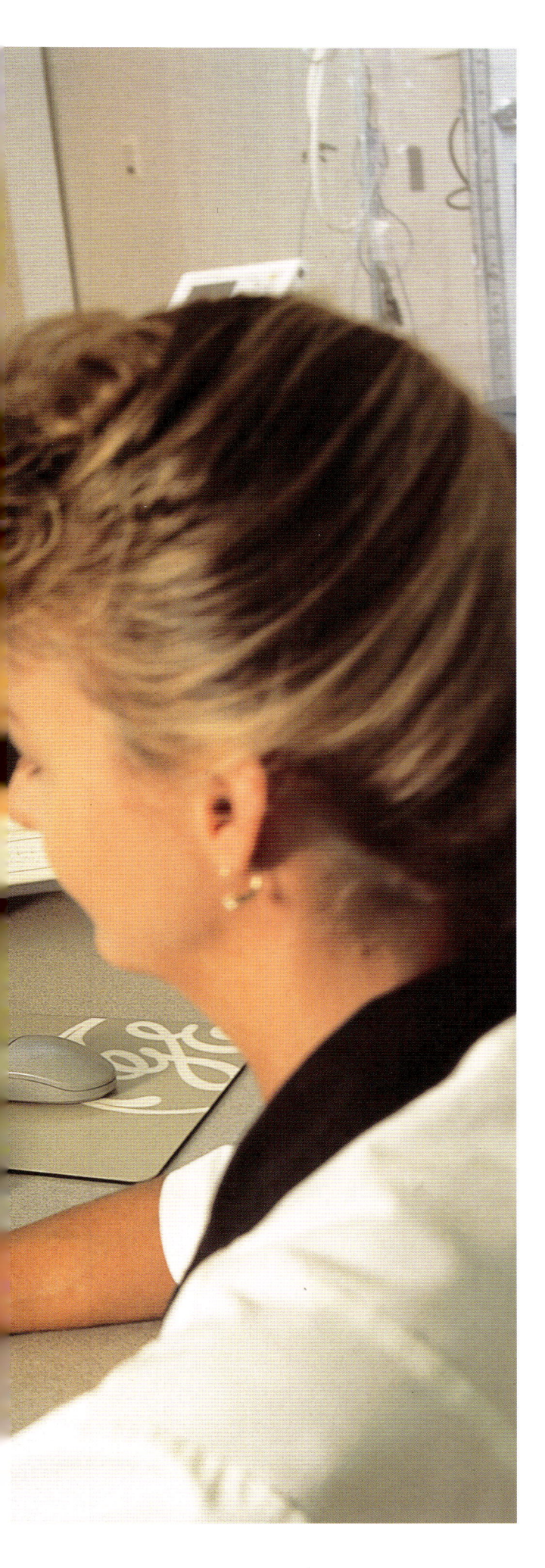

Chapter Eight

*Modern Health Care With
An Old-Fashioned Touch*

Loudoun's health care facilities are committed to placing patients before politics. Physicians and health care workers in the county are sensitive to the needs of their patients and never lose sight of the human aspect of treating people. Residents are afforded the highest standard of health care and a wide scope of health care services. The high caliber of physicians available to Loudoun County residents is unsurpassed. The two major hospitals utilized by Loudoun residents are Loudoun Hospital Center, part of the Loudoun Healthcare Network, and Reston Hospital Center, part of Columbia/HCA Healthcare System. Each hospital has a unique presence in the community.

◢

More than 85 years ago, Loudoun Hospital opened its doors in downtown Leesburg. The hospital quickly understood the importance of continually reevaluating the community's needs and, within six years, relocated to the 23-acre campus on Cornwall Street. This facility currently houses the hospital's long-term care center, rehabilitation services, and behavioral health residential services. Photo by David Galen.

Loudoun

Sunrise Assisted Living Centers are available throughout the county. This retirement community is designed with the intent of creating a warm, home-like atmosphere, while providing continual geriatric services, activities, and social events. Photo by David Galen.

Loudoun Hospital Center has experienced myriad growing pains in unison with the county's expansion. More than 85 years ago, the hospital opened its doors in a modest six-room brick building in downtown Leesburg. The hospital quickly understood the importance of continually reevaluating the community's needs and, within six years, relocated to the 23-acre campus on Cornwall Street in Leesburg. This facility currently houses the hospital's long-term care center, rehabilitation services, and behavioral health residential services. The hospital is exploring possible redevelopment of the campus as it anticipates an increasing demand for comprehensive geriatric programs. The hospital believes it is an ideal location for a full-service geriatric care facility. The facility could potentially include assisted and independent living quarters, subacute and acute nursing care, and long-term care.

In 1998, Loudoun Healthcare constructed a new 50-acre campus at Lansdowne east of Leesburg. The hospital is annexed with a new medical office building for the hospital's physicians. The new location has enhanced the hospital's visibility and availability to county residents. Close to 400 physicians hold privileges at the hospital and offer a wide range of medical services to the community.

In keeping with the tremendous surge of young families in Loudoun, the hospital's maternity and neonatology services are renowned. Complementing these services are childbirth and parent education courses. Despite the rapid growth, Loudoun Hospital has remained dedicated to the community's health care needs. High quality, compassionate care has remained first and foremost for the hospital.

As a system, Loudoun Healthcare considers the needs of the entire community. Community health care needs are continually studied and reevaluated. The hospital represents all medical specialities. The Cancer Care Center at Countryside in Sterling treats patients through chemotherapy and radiation oncology treatments. Support groups are available to patients and their families as

In keeping with the tremendous surge of young families in the county, Loudoun Hospital's maternity and neonatology services are renowned. Complementing these services are childbirth and parent education courses. Photo by David Galen.

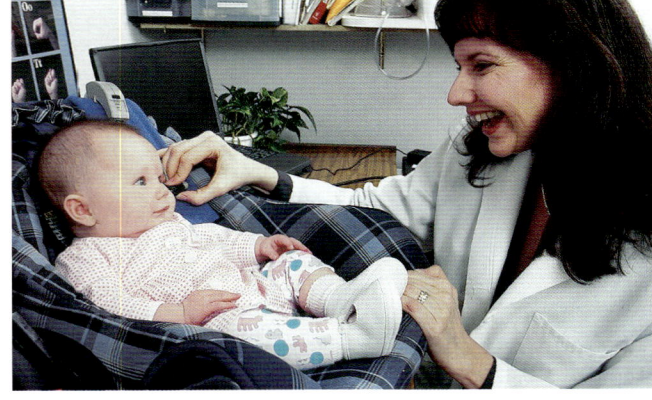

well. The Countryside location is also outfitted with an Ambulatory Surgery Center. The center offers a full range of outpatient services. High quality diagnostic imaging services include the two Magnetic Resonance Imaging (MRIs) devices in the county. The MRI located within the hospital is an enhanced MRI, elevating the patient's comfort level.

Loudoun Hospital Center offers ancillary services through NOVA Urgent Care in Sterling and Purcellville Urgent Care in the western portion of the county. As a community-based, nonprofit facility, Loudoun Hospital provides residents with several informational tools through the Health Resource Center. Residents may obtain information on local physicians and insurance plans accepted by those physicians through Physician Referral. The Health Information Library and Loudoun Healthcare web site allow individuals to research a variety of health care topics. The Hospice of Northern Virginia assists terminally ill patients and their families. Nursing home, as well as in-home care, is available with the assistance of hospital social workers, therapists, chaplains, and nonclinical volunteers. Bereavement counseling and caregiver support groups further solidify the outstanding resources offered by the hospital.

Loudoun Hospital Center's Gala Committee is dedicated to raising funds for the hospital. A new mobile health unit is the result of the committee's dedication. The unit, custom designed to the hospital's specifications, provides health and wellness screenings, as well as health education to the community. Loudoun Healthcare is working in collaboration with a number of Loudoun agencies and organizations to deliver curbside health care. Senior programs and community centers also benefit from the unit. The unit supports Mother Net by furnishing maternity and related services to women in need.

Loudoun Hospital Center continues its long-standing relationship with Monroe Technology Center. Student nurses from Monroe's Practical Nursing School attend sessions at the hospital's clinical training site and utilize the expertise of the hospital staff.

Loudoun Healthcare's mission is to provide unparalleled health care and education services to all Loudoun residents regardless of their ability to pay. The hospital rises to meet the challenge of the county's ever changing health care needs, while steadfastly maintaining its compassion and focus on the patient. The hospital upholds its tradition as a nonprofit, community hospital, locally governed and directed. High quality care, coupled with a dedicated staff of local residents, enriches the "patient first" philosophy. Loudoun Healthcare is unwavering in its commitment to the patient, despite changes in health care reform and management. As active, dedicated members of the community, an open line of communication and

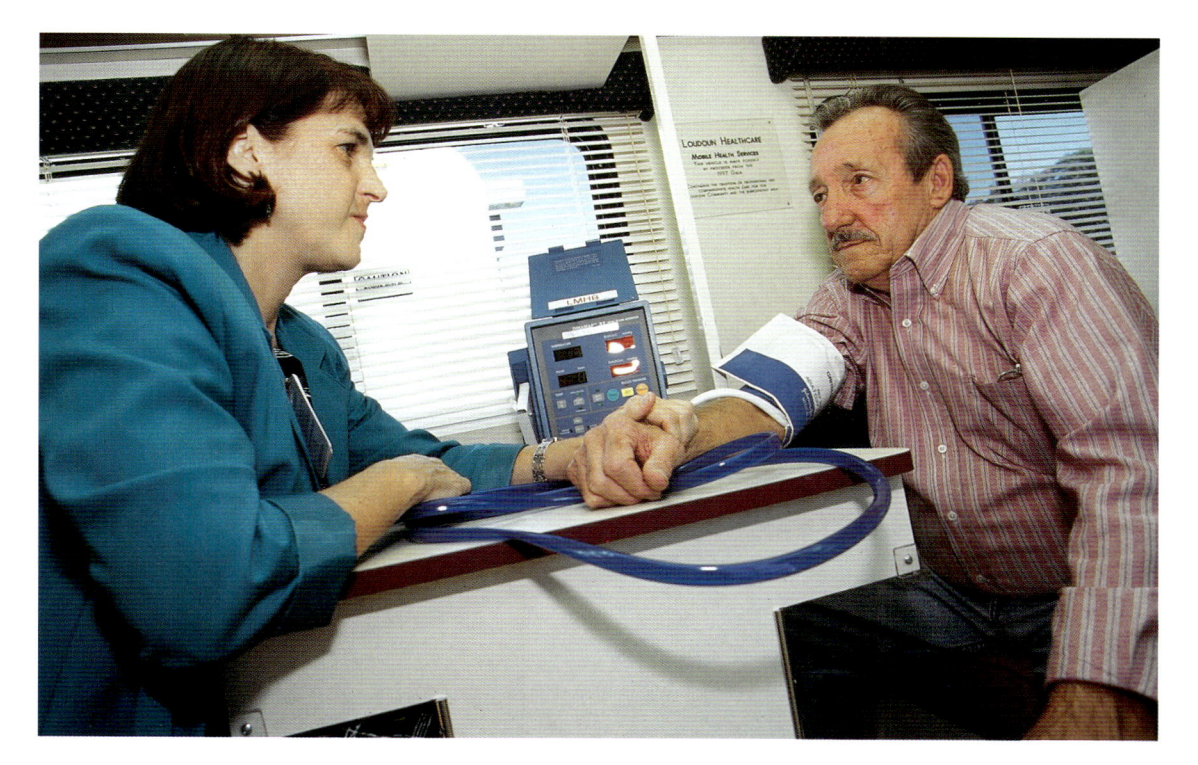

Loudoun Hospital's mobile health unit, custom designed to the hospital's specifications, provides health and wellness screenings, as well as health education, to the community. Loudoun Healthcare is working in collaboration with a number of Loudoun agencies and organizations to deliver curbside health care. Photo by David Galen.

Reston Hospital Center, established in 1986 to serve western Fairfax and eastern Loudoun Counties, offers a full range of medical services, including an extensive surgical department that specializes in outpatient surgery. Photo by David Galen.

trust between the hospital and residents allows Loudoun Healthcare to consistently evaluate, amend, and improve its services.

Although Reston Hospital Center is located in Fairfax County, many Loudoun residents and physicians utilize its facilities and services. The private hospital was established in 1986 to serve western Fairfax and eastern Loudoun Counties. More than 750 physicians have privileges at the hospital, and approximately 175 have offices on the hospital campus. Reston Hospital Center offers a full range of medical services. It is a medical-surgical hospital with an extensive surgical department, specializing in outpatient surgery. Approximately 80 percent of Reston's surgeries are performed as "same-day surgeries." Tremendous regional development has prompted significant expansion in the hospital's maternity center, which continues to grow each year. With the addition of a state-of-the-art radiation oncology department, Reston Hospital has become a true cancer care center. By providing all the necessary components of cancer care, including surgery, chemotherapy, and radiation therapy, in one centralized location, the patient's stress is alleviated and unnecessary travel reduced.

Reston Hospital Center realizes its patients are well-educated and expect the very best in medical care. With this in mind, the hospital continues to fine-tune many departments. The Urology Center, for example, is well-developed. Its state-of-the-art lithotripter, used to break up kidney stones, eliminates surgery and extensive recovery time for the patient. Rehabilitative and orthopedic medicine are also prominent hospital services. Physical therapy with a medically supervised fitness center round off the services available.

Reston Hospital Center is solidly entrenched in the community. Its highly credentialed, professional staff is comprised of local residents caring for their neighbors. It is an efficiently run medical facility, compassionate in its approach to care. With rapid regional growth, the hospital affords a sophisticated population to draw from an exceptional roster of physicians.

An extension of Reston's "neighbors caring for neighbors" policy is its community involvement. During the past four years, the hospital has been active in Healthy Community 2000, offering free or low-cost screenings for early detection of illness. The hospital has witnessed an increase in the number of corporations desiring health fairs for their employees. More than 200 men, women, and teens volunteer their time at the hospital, and the hospital's Senior Friends program for those over the age of 50 boasts a membership of 850. Two area high schools enjoy the benefit of hospital involvement. An Ethics Day, held annually, provides students with an opportunity to work through medical ethics dilemmas. Hospital nurses facilitate the process.

The hospital continually works to improve its level of service. To meet the demands of an expanding patient base, the 127-bed hospital is planning a building expansion to streamline key services such as maternity care and surgical services, as well as offer private room care throughout the hospital without adding more beds. With its commitment to the community, state-of-the-art equipment, and fine health care professionals, Reston Hospital Center is well-prepared to meet the community's needs into the next century.

Piedmont Behavioral Health Center and Graydon Manor are two area behavioral treatment centers. Piedmont serves adolescents and adults through its inpatient residential services. It treats substance abuse, a variety of mental disorders, and offers a private day school for grades 6 through 12. Graydon is a private, nonprofit residential hospital for adolescents and children with an array of emotional disorders. A course of treatments including education, group living, psychotherapy, and psychiatric services enables patients to function within the community at large. Outpatient services, individual, group, family, and chemical dependency therapies are available as well.

Assisted living centers are available to the community. Sunrise Assisted Living Centers are available throughout the county. This retirement community is designed with the intent of creating a warm, home-like atmosphere, while providing continual geriatric services, activities, and social events. Heritage Hall, in Leesburg, is a nursing care facility providing modern health care in a nurturing environment.

Blue Ridge Speech and Hearing Center is a nonprofit organization assisting hearing and speech impaired county residents and their families. It offers screening, evaluation, and therapy for hearing, speech, and language. NOVA West-Self Help for the Hard of Hearing is a support group for those with hearing loss.

Loudoun's equine heritage is apparent in the preeminent health care services available at the Marion duPont Scott Equine Medical Center at Morven Park. As the only facility with a sole emphasis on equine diagnostics and treatment, this veterinary teaching hospital has been treating horses for over 15 years. The 200 acres encompassing the center were donated by the Westmoreland Davis Memorial Foundation. A sizable bequest of $4 million from the late Marion duPont Scott, as well as private funding, led to the construction of this exquisite facility.

The center's strong relationship with Virginia Tech's Regional College of Veterinary Medicine facilitates the comprehensive range of veterinary teaching, research, and service offered to patients. A majority of its practice focuses on sports medicine and emergency medicine, particularly after-hours emergencies. With 20 on-site veterinarians servicing 3,000 horses each year, the center is outfitted with two operating rooms, 24 regular and 5 intensive care stalls, radiology, lab testing, video conferencing, and a pharmacy. With a steady increase in patients, the center is in the process of constructing additional facilities, including a state-of-the-art isolation facility, new emergency critical care, a veterinary learning center, and a high-speed exercise/stress test treadmill. Admissions cover a broad range of patients, including thoroughbreds, steeplechasers, hunter/show, and recreational horses from Pennsylvania to Florida. The center is unique in its public-private sector relationship. Clearly, the dedicated staff of more than 100 and its core of dedicated volunteers have successfully and ardently sustained the center.

Community awareness is the touchstone all of these facilities use to refine health care services. Loudoun County is comprised of extremely well-educated citizens. They are well aware of their health care options and are encouraged by these facilities to be more proactive in their health care. Health care in Loudoun County embodies the blend of tradition and innovation. It is ever changing in its technological advances, yet remains loyal to the human aspect of medicine. Residents can be assured they will receive modern health care with an old-fashioned touch.

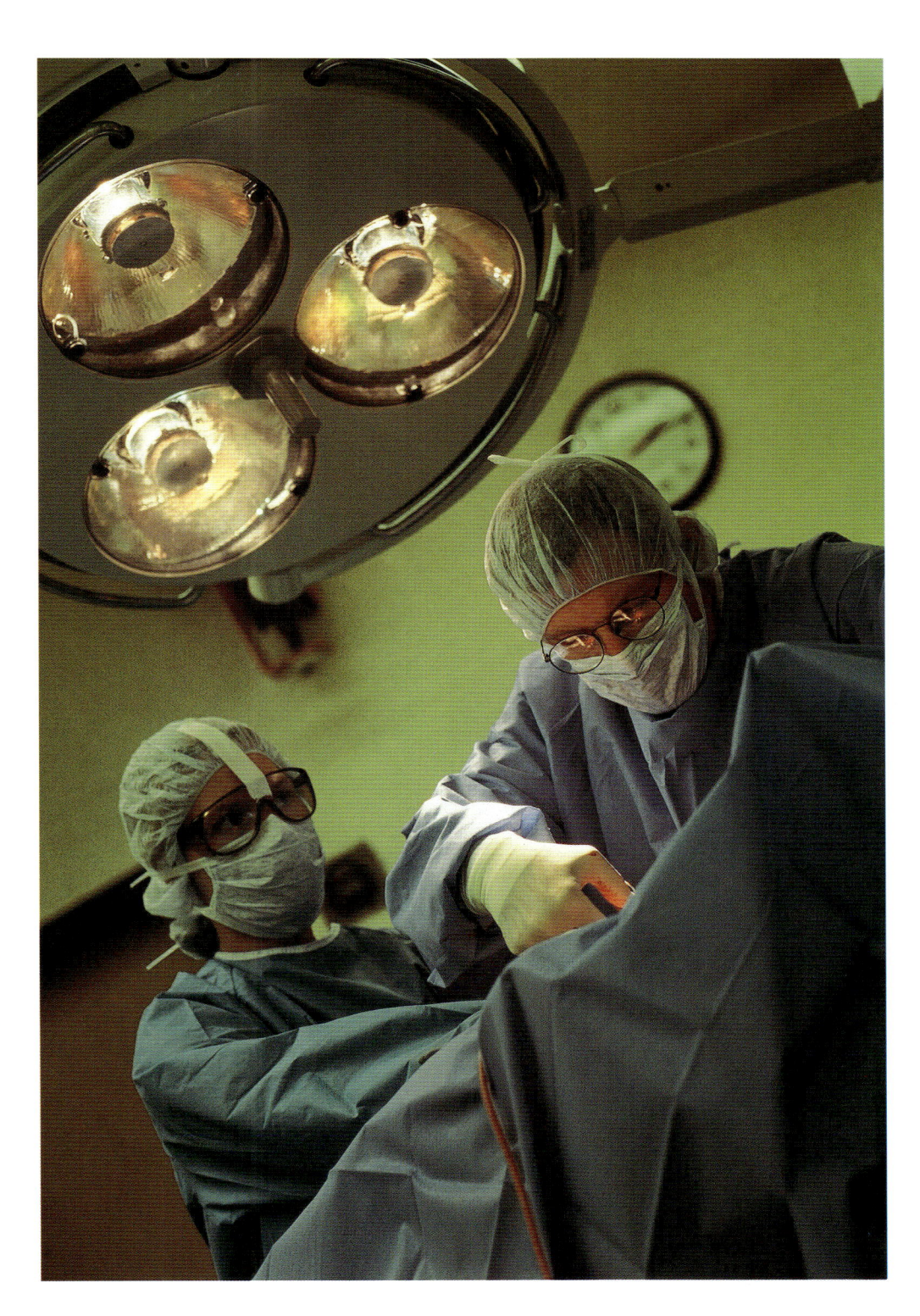

High quality care, coupled with a dedicated staff of local residents, enriches the "patient first" philosophy. Photo by David Galen.

69

Loudoun

Blending Tradition With Innovation

Chapter Nine

*Moving Toward the Future,
While Preserving the Past*

Loudoun County residents, businesses, and local officials have a vested interest in moving forward, while preserving the integrity of the past. Loudouners are united in their vision and remain resolute in their commitment to blend tradition with innovation well into the twenty-first century.

What makes Loudoun County special is an expansive and eclectic blend of histories, ideas, and values. All are working to blend the rural simplicity with the ever-changing technological complexities it faces. Photo by David Galen.

Loudoun

$\mathcal{L}$oudoun projects an alluring dichotomy. It is a modern, technologically advanced community of tomorrow, as well as a charming and reverent reminder of the past. The region successfully blends these two worlds to create an atmosphere conducive to a thriving economy, committed government body, excellent school system, and a strong, dedicated community.

While Loudoun continues to preserve the traditions and land that have strengthened and sustained it for centuries, it is keenly aware of the necessity to continually reevaluate the county's progress and direction. Collectively, the community understands this delicate balance and uses its foresight, talent, time, and dedication to act in the best interests of all Loudouners.

The Rural Economic Development Task Force, comprised of members of the Loudoun community, has detailed an array of innovative measures to boost farming and slow the westward movement of sprawl. One plan moving forward is the purchase of development rights on farmland. The Task Force also believes encouragement of leasing unused farmland for agricultural purposes will preserve part of the county's acreage. The Task Force encourages programs

(top) Oatlands Plantation, a Greek revival mansion, has breathtaking views and a spectacular formal garden. The garden's design was inspired from the centuries-old gardens of Italy and England. Photo by David Galen.

(right) Loudoun has created an atmosphere conducive to a thriving economy, committed government body, excellent school system, and a strong, dedicated community. Photo by David Galen.

such as Loudoun 4-H and Future Farmers of America to inspire the county's youngsters to carry on the farming tradition.

The horse industry continues to grow in Loudoun and is conducive to land conservation, both from an aesthetic and agricultural standpoint. It is a major economic force in Loudoun's rural economy, generating millions of dollars for the county. The Task Force wants to ensure the viability of the horse industry by creating more facilities for horse breeders and riders. The availability of equine facilities is one method proposed to spur land preservation. Further validation of this lucrative industry can be found in the plethora of equine events held here annually. These events, such as steeplechases, shows, stable tours, and point-to-point races, bolster tourism and financial stability in the county.

Farmers are stepping up efforts to preserve and strengthen their livelihoods. Local farmers are creating an alliance to fortify and enhance their resources and income through increased marketing endeavors. Loudoun farmers are attuned to the importance of blending traditional farming with technological advances. Agricultural preservation is envisioned through a farmers' web site as well. This site would link farmers' goods and services to horse breeders and owners in need of supplies and services such as bush hogging, hay, and straw.

Produce farmers understand the demand for fresh, high quality fruits and vegetables from those residing in urban and suburban areas of the region. As the demand for organic products increases among consumers, this faction of the agricultural industry will also expand in the county. Several local farmers are currently producing organically grown products for this developing market. Loudoun also has several cattle farmers, who can fulfill the demand for beef products.

Following the farmers' lead are wine makers and grape growers. There is a campaign among the county's wine makers and grape growers to identify Loudoun as a national, and possibly international, wine region. The group is optimistic its efforts will engender Loudoun's wine region to have recognition similar to California's wine country. Giving Loudoun wines an easily identifiable name among the wine industry and connoisseurs is a top priority of the group. A fitting and easily recognized name will boost tourism and revenue for the county. Likewise, further opportunity to promote conservation of farmland would be a direct benefit of this industry.

The Rural Task Force also believes there is a viable market for genetically engineered pharmaceuticals through biotechnology. Loudoun's proximity to the nation's capital would make it ideal for demonstration sites. With the presence of several prominent technology corporations and universities, the potential for high revenues and support in this field is very real. Traditional farming can no longer sustain the county's land without the aid of technology.

Christmas tree producers and nurseries also have a significant interest in preserving the county's land. Both industries are in high demand and generate solid income for the county. With the boom in new housing, large landscape trees and shrubs are needed.

The county is also investigating incentives to promote and support the preservation and renovation of farm buildings and structures with an eye toward maintaining Loudoun's rural character and ensuring availability for future agricultural use. Moreover, by-right uses in agriculturally zoned areas need further review to allow for adaptable uses to existing, albeit vacant, farm buildings and land. Nurseries, antique shops, restaurants, and craft shops are a few of the Task Force's suggestions.

Furthering the cause to maintain Loudoun's aesthetic quality is tourism. The county's tourism

Farmers are stepping up efforts to preserve and strengthen their livelihoods by creating an alliance to fortify and enhance their resources and income through increased marketing endeavors. Photo by David Galen.

Loudoun

Loudoun is a modern, technologically advanced world of tomorrow, as well as a charming and reverent reminder of the past. Photo by David Galen.

dollars rely heavily on the bucolic appeal of Loudoun's towns and countryside, particularly in the western portion of the county. Many corporations, small, and home-based businesses have set down roots in Loudoun due, in large part, to the magnetic appeal of the setting. In fact, many campuses contribute to land conservation through the purchase of large parcels, much of which remains open. Several have preserved wetlands, meadows, and wildlife in an effort to integrate their facilities into the landscape naturally.

With the recent introduction of national retail and discount stores has come a renewed vitality in many of the county's downtown centers. Shoppers enjoy side trips through the county's quaint towns and villages. First-class restaurants, specialty shops, and a plethora of cultural events beckon an increasing number of urban visitors. Changes will come as the county constantly seeks creative solutions, while remaining true to its values.

In a similar vein, Loudoun's burgeoning demand for conference centers has given way to a new industry. Some residents and businesses concerned with sprawl and lack of business meeting centers are purchasing estates and farms and converting them to rural conference centers like Wheatlands. The land remains intact, while the property's structures are renovated for meeting purposes. Several historic homes and buildings in towns like Leesburg are following this trend with new conference centers such as the historic Thomas Birkby House. The Task Force believes support of local bed-and-breakfasts and hotels will complement these facilities. A healthy income from businesses using these centers adds to the financial strength of the county and gives tourists and business travelers greater accessibility to the area.

Loudoun's residential growth is balanced with the Open Space Advisory Committee. The committee is mindful of the value of land preservation when developing. Many local builders and developers are creating subdivisions like Trevor Hill Plantation and Birch Hollow. The former, located north of Waterford, is Loudoun's original 10-acre cluster subdivision, while the latter is the county's first authentic hamlet. Towns such as Waterford are consciously supporting land conservation

The integration of architecture and technology adds to the attractiveness and fortitude of Loudoun County. It is a visual symbol of Loudoun's deepest values of paying homage to the past and simultaneously looking toward the future with a clear, conscientious, and hopeful vision. Photo by David Galen.

through the purchase of the land surrounding their tranquil villages. Many concerned citizens believe land preservation will occur when regulatory changes are made. Traditionally, land usage focused on urban and suburban development versus rural preservation. With this in mind, the Task Force believes tighter regulation of residential development will curb unnecessary destruction of the rural countryside. In developing neighborhoods, clustering homes will make way for more open space. The benefit is two-fold. The development gains a common area, while the horizon remains visually open and appealing. Developments such as Trevor Hill and Birch Hollow consider the outcome prior to building and, as a result, preserve many natural wildlife sanctuaries. Without considering these resources, Loudoun will lose its greatest asset—its naturally beautiful landscape. Tourism, in turn, will also feel the effects of overdevelopment, costing the county a substantial revenue stream. The Task Force is considering the creation of an ombudsman for farm owners. Funded by the county, the ombudsman would be the farmer's advocate in dealing with currently restrictive farm regulation.

The issue of rural preservation is reaching a crescendo among many Loudoun residents, and the need for a vocal rural task force is imperative if the county is to retain its aesthetic appeal. The independence, passion, and foresight characteristic to Loudoun will prevail. Eastern and western Loudouners are united in the commitment to champion the county's rural landscape, now and for the future.

Furthermore, the integration of architecture and technology adds to the attractiveness and fortitude of Loudoun County. It is a visual symbol of Loudoun's deepest values of paying homage to the past and simultaneously looking toward the future with a clear, conscientious, and hopeful vision. The key is to maintain equilibrium among the county's institutions, large corporations, and smaller businesses like bed-and-breakfasts, horse and cattle farms, produce farmers, and vineyards. It is what makes Loudoun County special—an expansive and eclectic blend of histories, ideas, and values. Loudoun is working to blend the rural simplicity with the ever-changing technological complexities it faces.

The county's tourism dollars rely heavily on the bucolic appeal of Loudoun's towns and countryside, particularly in the western portion of the county. Photo by David Galen.

Loudoun

Blending Tradition With Innovation

Chapter Ten

Networks and Technology

America Online, Inc., 78-81
United Airlines, 82-83
The Loudoun Times-Mirror, 84-85
Atlantic Coast Airlines, 86-87
Telos Corporation, 88
Enterworks, Inc., 89
Washington Dulles International Airport, 90
Loudoun County Transportation Association, 91
WAGE, AM 1200, 92

Loudoun County's communications and transportation firms keep information, people, and products circulating inside and outside the area. Photo by Victoria Cooper for AOL.

77

Loudoun

America Online, Inc.

With more than 20 million and 2 million worldwide members, respectively, America Online and CompuServe lead the consumer Internet space with nearly 50 percent of all users.

AOL is not just an online community—the socially responsible AOL mission and vision are designed to make a positive difference in communities across the nation.

America Online, Inc., known around the globe as AOL, is the number one Internet online service in the world—and it calls Loudoun County home. AOL is unquestionably one of the architects of eastern Loudoun's transformation into the nation's Internet capital. Under the leadership of Chairman and CEO Steve Case and President and Chief Operating Officer Bob Pittman, AOL has built a far-reaching family of multibrand media interactive services, Internet technologies, web brands, and e-commerce services—a multibillion-dollar success story.

AOL corporate headquarters sits on 155 acres of rolling Virginia countryside near Washington Dulles International Airport. Founded in 1985 and previously based in adjacent Fairfax County, Virginia, AOL chose Loudoun County as its new home in 1996. Its 772,000 square feet make it one of Loudoun's largest physical plants, and two buildings adding another 600,000 were under construction at the end of 1999. More than 2,500 employees of AOL's total workforce of 12,800 work at Dulles.

Among its business divisions are two worldwide Internet services, America Online and CompuServe. With more than 21 million and 2 million worldwide members, respectively, they lead the consumer Internet space with nearly 50 percent of all users. AOL's Interactive Services Group, which operates the online services, also manages Netscape Netcenter and Netscape Navigator and Communicator browsers. (The Netscape operations were acquired in early 1999.)

AOL's user-friendly format and worldwide community have changed the way people communicate, work, and play. With members averaging nearly an hour a day online, AOL has attracted more than 1,000 advertising, e-commerce, and content partners. AOL Keywords—more than 46,000 of them—whisk members to the information they seek. Message boards and chat rooms provide lively connections for members, and up-to-the-minute news from respected sources keeps them informed. They can even monitor the effectiveness of their elected representatives in the MyGovernment section. Additional AOL membership benefits include competitively priced products and services, such as long-distance plans, low interest Visa cards, and discounted travel bookings and car sales.

The familiar "You've Got Mail" announces messages via the world's most popular e-mail service; the phrase even achieved celebrity status as the title of a hit movie. And AOL's popular Instant Message feature allows users to see when their friends and family members are online and conduct real-time conversations with more than 70 million other people around the world.

For those who want to track and manage their finances, AOL provides the most visited finance area in cyberspace. It serves up more than 150 million stock quotes each day. Members are a click away from premier brokerages and AOL's banking partners, including Bank of America, Citibank,

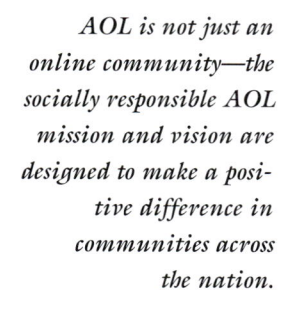

Wells Fargo, and Union Bank of California. AOL also helps members take responsibility for their health through numerous partner-resources like the Mayo Clinic and DrKoop.com. AOL's health pages aid members in ordering prescriptions, communicating with health care professionals, and researching personal and timely health questions.

Immensely popular AOL travel features give members easy access to destination information, planning, and online reservations through Travelocity.com and other services. Keeping up with sports and entertainment is easy with content provided by AOL partners like *People Magazine*, *Entertainment Weekly*, *TV Guide*, CBS Sportline, and Athlete Direct. And only AOL can bring together live online special events with the biggest names in sports, entertainment, and politics. The Dalai Lama, Michael Jordan, General Colin Powell, and First Lady Hillary Rodham Clinton have been AOL's special guests.

A special Kids Only Channel gives children a secure and monitored service designed just for them—with games, activities, clubs, and even help with homework. And AOL empowers parents through a wide range of safety features called Parental Controls that are built into the service and can be used to limit a child's access to the web, e-mail, and Instant Message features.

AOL 5.0, released in late 1999, further integrates the Internet experience into members' daily lives. Offering a more personalized presentation and immediate access to AOL's most popular attractions, it includes added features such as an interactive calendar, a powerful next-generation search engine, and easy e-mail photos through "You've Got Pictures," developed in partnership with Kodak. AOL 5.0 is designed to work at any connection speed and supports new technologies like DSL, cable modems, and satellite broadband connectivity.

AOL's Interactive Properties Group builds and acquires branded properties for multiple services and platforms. Digital City is a community-based web site that blends information with expert opinion and local-user insights to help people get more out of their communities. City-specific sites cover locally relevant news, job markets, entertainment, and shopping. The growing list of Digital City sites reached 60 as 1999 ended.

AOL's planned acquisition of MapQuest.com—announced in late 1999—will provide its members and users across the Web with award-winning maps and directions from the world's leading provider of maps on the Internet.

With 50 million registrants worldwide and millions more joining each month, ICQ is a communications service that supports real-time message exchange with friends across the Internet. With more than two-thirds of all users outside the United States, ICQ has become the world's most popular communication portal.

AOL MovieFone is America's largest movie listing guide and ticketing service. With a simple phone call or a visit to moviefone.com, the cinema savvy can know what is playing and purchase their tickets online without having to wait in line.

AOL's Netscape Enterprise Group operates the strategic e-commerce alliance—sold under the iPlanet brand name—in partnership with Sun

AOL corporate headquarters sits on 155 acres of rolling Virginia countryside near Washington Dulles International Airport. Photo by Jeff Goldberg/ Esto.

AOL has built a far-reaching family of multibrand media interactive services, Internet technologies, web brands, and e-commerce services—a multibillion-dollar success story.

Microsystems. By helping companies put their business online, they are prime movers in America's new economy. This unique alliance offers comprehensive end-to-end solutions for globally accessible e-commerce businesses—strategically significant since $3.2 trillion in Internet commerce will be conducted by 2003, according to Forrester Research.

Outside the United States, AOL International operates its branded Internet services in 15 countries and 7 languages; it launched AOL Hong Kong and AOL Brazil in the last half of 1999. AOL and CompuServe services include more than 3 million members outside the United States. Through AOLNet, AOLGlobalnet, and other networks, America Online offers the largest dial-up network in the world to ensure access in more than 1,500 cities in over 100 countries.

In January 2000, AOL announced a merger with Time Warner. The merger brings together the world's number one Internet company and the world's number one media company to offer consumers a range of unprecedented services and brands. The merged company, named AOL Time Warner Inc., will be the premier global company delivering branded information, entertainment, and communications services across rapidly converging media platforms.

AOL is not just an online community—the socially responsible AOL mission and vision are designed to make a positive difference in communities across the nation. The AOL Foundation was established in 1997 to foster the use of online technology to benefit society, improve the lives of families and children, and empower the disadvantaged. Foundation programs are national in scope, and special emphasis is placed on using the online medium to benefit communities in which AOL offices are located. The Foundation is helping to bring the digital age to low-resource communities, organizations, and schools in the Washington, D.C./Virginia region, where AOL and the Foundation are based. Through the AOL Achievers program, Civic Involvement Initiative Grants, the Executive Leadership Program (with Greater DC Cares), and the Interactive Education Initiative, the AOL Foundation is helping to shape the future of its local community. The Foundation's many recent grant recipients include Habitat for Humanity, Martha's Table, the Bright Beginnings program for

America Online employees work in the supercharged atmosphere of a world-changing enterprise. The company is known for providing a casual but challenging work environment that places a value on family, education, and quality of life.

homeless preschoolers, the Humane Society of Loudoun County, and AOL's neighboring Ashburn Fire and Rescue Company.

AOL has introduced a mentoring program with local elementary schools and a workforce training partnership with a local college. To promote the arts, Holiday@AOL showcases the artwork of Loudoun County students. AOL is also a corporate sponsor of many charitable events, such as the AIDS Walk on Washington, and encourages volunteerism and charitable giving among its employees through its Giving Tree service.

America Online employees work in the supercharged atmosphere of a world-changing enterprise. The company is known for providing a casual but challenging work environment that places a value on family, education, and quality of life. AOL believes that employees can have fun while taking ownership of what they do, and at AOL, ownership is not just a word to enhance productivity. Employees become owners through a stock purchase program, broad-based stock options, and opportunities to earn additional stock based on performance. "We're glad we've been able to create wealth both within the region and for our employees," says an AOL spokesperson. AOL's efforts were recognized in 2000 by its listing on *Fortune* magazine's "100 Best Companies to Work For in America."

AOL and its visionary CEO Steve Case look forward to aggressive participation in the new millennium economy. Perhaps nowhere is the economy's impact more visible than in the entrepreneurial culture of the Washington area, and especially in Loudoun County, the center of the information revolution. Case believes that the success of the region as a community will be determined by the collaboration and innovation of the new century's first few years, using the wealth of resources and working together to build a new generation of economic leaders.

Addressing 1999's Potomac Conference to link the interests of business and community, Case urged broad cooperation to demonstrate the power of information technology, especially the Internet, for improving communities, education, and government. "What I believe," said Case, "and what most business and civic leaders in successful regions have learned, is this: you cannot have a strong economy without a strong community—they go hand in hand. Successful regions are built by teams of civic leaders who collaborate to build a strong community that can support a dynamic economy." To do this, he advocates a continuing regional dialogue.

AOL is active in the Northern Virginia Technology Council, the Loudoun County Chamber of Commerce, and other organizations that support good business and good communities. America Online, through its considerable economic impact and demonstrable civic responsibility, makes northern Virginia a better place to live.

America Online, Inc., known around the globe as AOL, is the number one Internet online service in the world— and it calls Loudoun County home. Photo by Omar Salinas/ Hi Tech Photo.

Loudoun

United Airlines

United Airlines, the largest air carrier in the world and the largest majority employee-owned company, operates its eastern hub at Washington Dulles International Airport in Loudoun County. Offering 2,300 flights system-wide each day to 139 destinations around the world, United recognizes Northern Virginia as one of the country's most dynamic business and residential centers and is making a significant investment in its economy and quality of life.

Amid United's fleet of Magnificent 777s, Mike Beirne, Washington metro area managing director, showcases the Boeing 777s, which emphasize the airline's vital corporate value of teamwork and its commitment to metro Washington and the Dulles corridor, making United Loudoun County's largest employer.

United's Dulles hub consists of over 360 daily domestic and international departures. The airline increased its daily departures from Dulles by more than 60 percent in the spring of 1999, giving area travelers the frequency and diversity of service only a major hub can offer. Adding to United's powerful presence at Dulles is its business relationship with Dulles-based Atlantic Coast Airlines, operating as United Express. United and United Express carry more than 70 percent of all Dulles passengers and United handles 40 percent of the cargo. Continuing expansion of hub services is key to United's long-term strategic plan.

Nonstop United flights departing from Dulles connect the area with 76 destinations, both domestic and international. United's Dulles hub serves as its premier trans-Atlantic gateway to 8 cities; its Star Alliance partnerships with Air Canada, Air New Zealand, All Nippon Airways, Ansett Australia, Lufthansa, SAS, Thai Airways International, and Varig extend United's reach, offering uninterrupted quality and convenience to more than 600 destinations around the globe. Long a favorite with business travelers, United has expanded services to the leisure travel market by initiating seasonal nonstop service from northern Virginia to St. Thomas, U.S. Virgin Islands.

Of critical importance to its business customers, United provides near-hourly service to Boston, New York LaGuardia, and frequent daily service to Los Angeles. More than five United nonstop flights each day connect Dulles with Atlanta, Chicago, Denver, Orlando, and San Francisco. Loudoun County's thriving corporate community—much of which depends on 24-hour-a-day, 7-day-a-week activity, can depend on United and its affiliates to meet its air travel needs.

With flight operations in Dulles' midfield C and D concourses, the airline operates 40 gates to speed passengers along their way. Three Red Carpet Club rooms, two First Class Lounges, a 1-K Lounge, and Special Services Counters enhance the travel experience for the many business travelers who sometimes seem to fly the friendly skies more than they sit at their desks.

The membership Red Carpet Clubs provide comfortable lounges with the necessary privacy to use Red Carpet phones and faxes, or to simply unwind between flights. Complimentary continental breakfasts and nonalcoholic beverages are served, with cocktails available at popular prices.

The United workforce numbers 100,000 nationwide, and 7,500 are employed at Dulles operations sites, including a cargo facility, ground maintenance, and a regional reservations center and sales office in nearby Sterling, Virginia. The Dulles Greenway offers Loudoun employees a pleasant, pastoral commute to the airport. The Loudoun County Chamber of Commerce estimates that more than 5,000 of United's workers live in the county, making the airline its largest employer.

Employee-owners Linda Roach and Wendy Van Clief at the Dulles Reservations Center in Sterling enthusiastically support their favorite charities with ongoing bake sales and fund-raising activities frequently backed by United corporate contributions. Through active community service and untold volunteer hours, United's 5,000 employees residing in Loudoun County greatly enhance the quality of life for their families and their community.

Blending Tradition With Innovation

The company's contribution to northern Virginia's economic vitality has not gone unnoticed. Says Virginia Governor Jim Gilmore of the recent expansion: "I have worked with United Airlines to explore how air service in the Commonwealth can be enhanced to improve economic activity here. This expansion is a tremendous validation of the important business and leisure markets in Virginia, which should attract more passengers and develop more markets."

U.S. Senator Charles Robb says that "United's commitment to expanded services at Washington Dulles is welcome news to Virginia's air travelers. The new flights offer consumers significantly more choices to and from Virginia."

But serving the region's transportation needs and making an undeniable financial impact on the Loudoun economy is not the end of the local United story. United Airlines is a company of global importance taking great pride in its civic leadership. Internationally consistent in it corporate value of community service, it is committed to supporting projects and programs that improve the quality of life in the communities it serves and where its employees live and work, encouraging management and staff to be actively involved in community service. Carol Brown, Sales Manager-Corporate Sales, is a member of the 1999 Loudoun County Chamber of Commerce board of directors, and other key managers serve on a variety of nonprofit boards that impact the area's human service and cultural life.

As the official airline for the Loudoun Healthcare Foundation's Annual Fall Gala, United helps raise funds to meet costly care for hospitalized patients and underwrites health-related community outreach. Loudoun Healthcare is an independent, locally controlled, not-for-profit health care organization whose mission is to provide quality, compassionate, and accessible health care to the entire Loudoun community. United's contributions have helped fund the Mobile Health Services, a 40-foot mobile unit dedicated to providing health care to the medically underserved in Loudoun County.

The airline supports ECHO—Every Citizen has Opportunities—providing community-based training, employment, and transportation services to Loudoun County's adult citizens with disabilities. In 1996, United was named the official airline of the Whitman-Walker Clinic in Washington, D.C., and northern Virginia, acting as a major sponsor of the clinic's many fund-raising efforts including AIDS Walk-Washington. In 1997, and again in 1999, United hosted the United Golf Classic, donating the entire proceeds to the clinic. Whitman-Walker serves persons with HIV/AIDS with outpatient medical and dental programs, case management, access to testing and medications, and education programs.

With an eye on the area's children, United has adopted Loudoun County's Sugarland, Meadowland, and Ashburn Elementary Schools, and supported Park View High School. United employees host an annual "Breakfast at the North Pole" for Loudoun's special education preschoolers at its Reservations Center in Sterling. It also is one of the biggest corporate supporters of Neediest Kids, Inc., an organization assisting at-risk children in the Washington area. Mike Beirne, United's managing director for the Washington metropolitan area, was awarded the 1999 Tom Cookerly Humanitarian Award by the Neediest Kids.

Grassroots support of favorite charities by metropolitan employee-owners provides direction for corporate sponsorships. United's strong tradition of community service is guided locally by the Volunteer Coordinator Network, a part of the global United We Care Corporate Volunteer Program. Employees at the Dulles Reservations Center in Sterling provide ongoing support for the American Heart Walk, Wednesday's Child, Habitat for Humanity, Help the Homeless, For the Love of Children (FLOC), and Fantasy Flight to the North Pole for critically ill youngsters, to name but a few of the many charities supported through bake sales, walkathons, and donations. United was recently honored in Washington with the prestigious Points of Light Award for Excellence in corporate community service.

United Airlines and Loudoun County create a synergy that is mutually beneficial. Each can be proud of its role in the other's success, and the partnership can look forward to a healthy future.

Customer service ranks high with seasoned United agents Terry Fix and Pat Collins, who share an easy camaraderie and help make the Sterling Ticket Office a favorite and convenient spot to be ticketed.

Serving Loudoun County and beyond holds double meaning for Loudoun Healthcare's Mobile Services Unit and United Airlines, which helps fund the Loudoun Healthcare Foundation and underwrites health-related community outreach services.

Loudoun

The Loudoun Times-Mirror

As the oldest newspaper in history-rich Loudoun County, *The Loudoun Times-Mirror* is accurately named. Loudoun's remarkable story has been reflected on its pages and those of its predecessors for more than 200 years, and amidst fast-paced change, this local paper remains committed to community journalism at its best. From its Market Street office in Leesburg, the weekly *Times-Mirror* covers the issues and events of the entire county.

Times-Mirror *Editor Martin Casey reviews an early copy of a press-run while the ink is still wet. The newspaper regularly publishes in four sections, each printed separately and combined for weekly distribution.*

Two centuries ago, a front page may have included stories about births, deaths, and the sale of cattle; these were the events that made a difference in the daily lives of readers. Today, the subject matter may be different, but the newspaper still focuses on what is important to readers rather than what is important to newsmakers. A current edition might delve into new discussions within the growing numbers of eastern county homeowners' associations or a high-tech program in the schools. But it will also skillfully cover some of the same issues it did years ago—zoning, taxes, water conservation, crop forecasts, local sports, and growth.

The editors believe that each issue must contain something that everyone can use. They keep the paper relevant to the rapidly growing population by responding to the interests of new, young families without Loudoun roots. Reading *The Times-Mirror* and discovering the heart and soul of Loudoun is one way newcomers become part of the community rather than mere observers.

The popular *Weekender* section focuses on entertainment and recreation. With a full rundown of enticing local happenings, it helps Loudoun residents make the most of their valuable leisure time. A very special event, like 1998's Babe Ruth World Series, may spark daily editions to feed the community's interest.

The paper also takes considerable responsibility for preserving those elements of community that are embraced by Loudoun natives. Writers from the county's towns and neighborhoods contribute to weekly columns about what's happening in their corner of the county. They document their neighbors' personal triumphs and children's achievements. They keep the hometown flavor alive.

Because many residents read daily papers from the nearby nation's capital and receive its broadcast media, *The Times-Mirror* chooses not to compete with detailed reporting on national affairs, concentrating instead on Loudoun's news. Staff journalists are local professionals who write for and about the people living and working in Loudoun County. Local news is not trivial news; the paper is particularly important in helping residents know about—and have a voice in—the complex issues that will shape their futures, such as the impacts or the county's environment and infrastructure. Examples of the paper's support for preservation and economic viability of Loudoun County's rural land are the recently produced historical document *Farming on the Edge* and the popular *Barns of Loudoun* poster.

The Times-Mirror has had a distinguished roster of publishers that include former Virginia Governor Westmoreland Davis, who ran the paper in the 1930s from his Morven Park estate. Now it is part of Times Community Newspapers, one of 16 published by Dulles-based ArCom Publishing, owned by northern Virginia's Arundel family.

But if any individual has typified the paper's community identity, it is the beloved Miss Fannie Reid. At the time of her death in 1994, after 73 years on the job, Miss Reid was the paper's associate publisher. A determined working woman ahead of her time, she began her career at age 21, taking the milk train each day from her Purcellville home. In later years she nabbed rides with co-workers and was at her desk every morning until a month before her death. The memory of Miss Reid's encyclopedic knowledge of the county and the newspaper industry is still revered. "She was a

Blending Tradition With Innovation

teacher of reporters, editors, and publishers, and was their Loudoun conscience," said Arthur Arundel after her death. "She leaves a powerful legacy of excellence in journalism and devotion to this Virginia county."

Evidence of the county's changes is seen in the paper's advertising. Once displaying only small businesses and retailers that dot the countryside, these advertisers have been joined by the regional and national retail chains that are recent Loudoun arrivals; a large upscale mall opened near Dulles in 1999. But the greatest change over time is in *The Times-Mirror's* production. From the early days of typed out copy and painstaking slugsetting to on-the-scene laptops that relay words and images via high-speed Internet lines, the paper is a study in the evolution of print journalism. In addition to its local editions, the Leesburg site prints all the other Times Community Newspapers.

The Loudoun Times-Mirror employs 125 people, and management makes every effort to support a family-style working atmosphere. Employee appreciation is evident in Super Bowl parties, quarterly luncheons, and just about anything else that makes work fun.

With the paper's management active in the Chamber of Commerce, Rotary, and other service organizations, *The Times-Mirror* carries out its community responsibilities in many ways. It established the Miss Reid Scholarship for female students interested in careers in journalism. To foster a generation of young newspaper readers, *The Times-Mirror* is distributed to every school in the county, and staff members conduct frequent tours of the newsroom and presses for interested classes.

The Times-Mirror has long been recognized for excellence in journalism. It has won the first place award of the Suburban Newspapers of America as well as the Virginia Press Association's top award for weekly newspapers. The quality and values of Loudoun County are reflected in the editorial standards of the paper. "A story can be true without being fair," noted Miss Reid years ago. *Times-Mirror* journalism is both.

As the county grows, *The Times-Mirror* continues to examine the best way it can serve the community. That may include more frequent publication, and it certainly includes increasing distribution, now at nearly 22,000. But as Miss Reid said, "there will always be a *Times-Mirror*. Its roots are too firm to loosen." ◪

The Times-Mirror office is in historic downtown Leesburg, directly across Market Street from the county courthouse, reflected here in the front windows. The newspaper traces its roots in Leesburg to 1798.

A pressman tends the 8-unit Goss Urbanite offset color press, put into operation September 26, 1989, that prints all 16 Times community newspapers weekly from the Leesburg plant. This is the seventh generation of press technology since an original Franklin single-sheet flatbed press in 1798.

Atlantic Coast Airlines

Established in 1989, Atlantic Coast Airlines now serves more than 50 destinations with over 550 departures each day—over 250 of them from Washington Dulles.

Atlantic Coast Airlines Holdings, Inc. is the nation's fastest-growing regional airline. The independent, publicly traded corporation (NASDAQ: ACAI) operates at Washington Dulles International Airport as United Express, one of six carriers in a comprehensive marketing agreement with United Airlines to provide convenient, high-quality air service. ACA is the exclusive United Express carrier on the East Coast.

The company is also beginning a new relationship with Delta Air Lines to offer jet service in markets throughout the eastern United States as part of the Delta Connection program.

Established in 1989, Atlantic Coast Airlines now serves more than 50 destinations with over 550 departures each day—over 250 of them from Washington Dulles. The airline established a new record in 1999 by carrying over 3 million passengers.

ACA also provides service to a number of cities from Chicago O'Hare International Airport, United's worldwide hub. Atlantic Coast Airlines' route system spans from Maine to Florida and as far west as the Dakotas.

The company is enjoying unprecedented success by any measure—from route expansion to passenger growth to financial performance. In a national climate of mergers, acquisitions, and restructuring, the airline has a remarkably solid management team—many key leaders have been with the company since its founding. Chairman and CEO Kerry Skeen is a noted Loudouner who has earned a reputation as a growth-oriented leader in the regional airline industry.

Now in its second decade of operation, the company is proud to be one of the leading employers in the Loudoun/Northern Virginia area—with a staff that is growing to 2,700 employees and beyond. And like other companies located in the high-tech Dulles Corridor, it continues to create new career opportunities for those with an interest in com-mercial aviation and the travel industry. ACA is the only airline headquartered at Washington Dulles, and offers full- and part-time positions, including flight attendants, customer service staff, aircraft support teams, operations personnel, administrative staff, sales and marketing professionals, and many other areas. All ACA personnel receive an excellent benefits package, including a profit sharing program and flight privileges. The company takes an active interest in promoting from within its own ranks and can boast of many managers and directors who started in other positions and accepted new challenges and responsibilities over time.

In addition to its extraordinary workforce, Atlantic Coast Airlines' success is due in large part to the introduction and expansion of its regional jet program, which has gained strong public acceptance. ACA is well on its way toward a future that will include a predominantly jet-oriented fleet—by acquiring an ever-growing number of 50-passenger Canadair Regional Jets (CRJs). These aircraft are faster, quieter, and more comfortable than the so-called "commuter planes" of the past, and add a new dimension to regional airline operations.

With the growth and buildup of Washington Dulles as the East Coast hub of the world's largest airline, ACA continues to be a major contributor to the economic vitality and increased overall passenger traffic there. Since a growing number of passengers use United Express as a connector to transcontinental and trans-Atlantic flights offered by United, that airline's move in 1999 to increase Dulles flights by 60 percent means concurrent

Blending Tradition With Innovation

United Express, operating at Washington Dulles International Airport, is one of six carriers in a comprehensive marketing agreement with United Airlines to provide convenient, high-quality air service. ACA is the exclusive United Express carrier on the East Coast.

Located in the high-tech Dulles Corridor, Atlantic Coast Airlines continues to create new career opportunities for those with an interest in commercial aviation and the travel industry.

growth for ACA. As of now, Dulles has eclipsed Reagan National Airport and Baltimore-Washington International as the most popular airport in the Washington metropolitan area.

The 1999 opening of the United Express concourse at Dulles marked another milestone in ACA's history. One of only a few terminals in the country dedicated to a single regional carrier, the 70,000-square-foot midfield terminal includes 12 gates with 36 aircraft positions, and offers a great number of upgraded amenities in a much more pleasant, relaxed atmosphere. Designated Concourse A, the United Express operation is literally at the center of all activity at Dulles—with direct mobile lounge service both to the main terminal as well as United connections at the C/D Concourse. Additional offerings include a food court/brew pub and an Executive Lounge for invited United Express guests.

Also located at Dulles is Atlantic Coast Airlines' maintenance facility, completed in 1998. The 90,000-square-foot physical plant is the only such maintenance installation at Dulles, and is an important factor in ACA's operational efficiency.

The airline has both benefited from and contributed to the explosive growth of the Dulles region. In fact, Loudoun County markets its air accessibility as a key feature to businesses seeking to relocate or expand their operations in this area. As Virginia's hometown airline, Atlantic Coast Airlines employs more than 2,700 people, the vast majority of whom live in Loudoun County. That makes ACA one of the county's top five employers. With active participation in Loudoun County's Economic Development Commission and the Loudoun County Chamber of Commerce, the airline is justifiably proud of its role in the county's business boom.

As Loudoun and Washington Dulles continue to prosper, so will Atlantic Coast Airlines—making it a company that is truly on the leading edge of growth in Loudoun County. ◢

TELOS® Corporation

Telos specializes in building information technology companies that leverage the Internet and enable the Business-to-Business (B2B) and Business-to-Government (B2G) e-marketplaces.

Telos® is a dynamic information technology corporation located in Ashburn, the heart of northern Virginia's high-tech corridor. Telos® specializes in building information technology companies that leverage the Internet and enable Business-to-Business (B2B) and Business-to-Government (B2G) e-marketplaces. Telos's® companies include Enterworks®, Xacta™, SecureTrade™, Telos®.com, and traditional Telos®.

Enterworks® is a leading provider of software for aggregating e-business content and automating e-business processes. Enterworks® solutions form a software superstructure that powers e-business portals and e-marketplaces. Its products access, aggregate, catalog, and deliver content and automate the business processes necessary to support, strengthen, and accelerate e-business interactions.

Xacta™ is an emerging e-commerce integrator providing B2B trusted e-marketplace solutions to global 2000 companies and emerging digital businesses. Xacta™ professionals architect, engineer, integrate, and support complex B2B e-marketplaces and extranets, focusing on security, reliability, scalability, and integration with existing systems and processes.

SecureTrade™ is an Application Service Provider (ASP) hosting B2B and B2G e-payment applications for developing countries. SecureTrade™ is initially focusing on the developing countries in the Association of Southeast Asian Nations (ASEAN) region. SecureTrade™ hosts applications that address real time trading, bill presentment and payment, and supply chain management. SecureTrade™'s proprietary network of customers, vendors, and banking institutions enables it to provide services on a subscription basis to execute, pay, and settle transactions in a virtual digital marketplace.

Telos®.com is an Application Service Provider (ASP) hosting B2G applications which deliver information technology products and services to the federal government and those working within the government procurement process. By applying business rules unique to the company, contract, or customers, the Telos®.com trusted e-marketplace allows customers and contractors to outsource their order enablement and order fulfillment process.

Traditional Telos® and services include network infrastructure products and related services such as contract software development, help desk support, LAN/WAN development, and systems and software engineering. Additionally, Telos® has developed business units dedicated to information security, wireless networking, enterprise management, enterprise integration, and messaging.

In 1999, Telos® companies realized approximately $185 million in revenues and employed approximately 1,100 associates worldwide. In 1995, Telos® chose Loudoun County as the site for its corporate headquarters because Loudoun County offers Telos® associates an exceptional quality of life and a challenging and progressive business environment. As an active member of the Loudoun County community, Telos associates have formed a School-Business Partnership with Broad Run High School. Through this partnership, Telos® has donated computers, helped set-up the school's information technology network, and provided Internet access. More important than simply providing equipment, the partnership allows Telos® associates the opportunity to work directly with students and teachers in software and web development instruction. In addition, Telos® supports its employees in their contributions to community volunteer programs, including the Community Holiday Coalition and other programs. Telos® works closely with George Washington University through its Corporate Liaison Program, is a member of the Loudoun County Chamber of Commerce, and is a corporate sponsor of George Washington University's Loudoun Environmental Indicators Project.

"Telos" is a registered trademark of Telos Corporation. "Enterworks" is a registered trademark of Enterworks, Inc. All other product, service, and company names are trademarks or registered trademarks of their respective owners.

Blending Tradition With Innovation

Enterworks, Inc.

Enterworks develops and markets software that integrates the data and automates the business processes behind Web portals and e-business marketplaces. Portals give a company's employees, customers, partners, and suppliers a single on-line location where they can find information, interact, perform transactions, and get support and service. E-marketplaces bring together buyers and suppliers in a content-rich, Web-based hub that offers efficient evaluation, comparison, and purchase of products and services, typically within a particular industry.

Established in 1996, Enterworks employs more than 170 people and is headquartered in Ashburn, Virginia. Loudoun County's record growth in the high-tech industry fuels the supply of visionary IT professionals that ensure Enterworks' continued success. Enterworks' customer support is based in Pasadena, California, and there are five other offices throughout the country.

Enterworks' products are targeted at companies that need to build competitive strengths by increasing their speed, agility, and business intelligence, but which are challenged by complex data environments and interwoven business processes. Enterworks focuses primarily on health care, manufacturing, and government markets, offering consulting, training, and customer and partner support services as part of a total solution for its customers. Enterworks' customers include Boeing, IBM/Tivoli, and the U.S. Army.

Enterworks' products reflect the reality that e-business involves more than simple transactions between businesses and their direct customers; full-scale e-business involves complex business-to-business *interactions* across extended enterprises comprised of employees, customers, partners, and suppliers connected through the Internet. Enterworks' products integrate data and business processes to support and strengthen these interactions. In addition, the products provide people with unified and tailored views of information and guide them through business processes.

Enterworks offers two principal products. Enterworks Content Integrator™ delivers to e-business portals and marketplaces an always up-to-date, customized catalog of information that is seamlessly integrated from multiple disparate data sources. Portal creators and marketplace operators can use Enterworks Content Integrator™ to quickly add information sources and integrate new suppliers with minimal effort.

Enterworks Process Integrator™ (EPI) integrates people, applications, and processes using the best practices and domain expertise of an enterprise. EPI automatically coordinates the flow of tasks and activities in any e-business process such as on-line order handling and problem solving. EPI ensures that the right people have the right information at the right time.

Enterworks' software products have been featured in numerous publications, including *Computerworld, Information Week, Inter@ctive Week, PC Week*, and *Software Magazine* Customers who use Enterworks' solutions have been recognized by the *Computerworld* Smithsonian Awards Program and the Center of Excellence for Information Technology. Enterworks Content Integrator™ recently earned *Industry Week's* 1999 Technology of the Year Award, an honor given to emerging technologies that "can make a difference in the global economy."

At Enterworks, as in Loudoun County, technology is the future, and the future is now.

Established in 1996 and headquartered in Ashburn, Enterworks develops and markets software that integrates the data and automates the business processes behind Web portals and e-business marketplaces.

"Enterworks" is a registered trademark, and "Enterworks Content Integrator" and "Enterworks Process Integrator" are trademarks of Enterworks, Inc. All other product, service, and company names are trademarks of their respective owners.

Washington Dulles International Airport

The distinctive Dulles Airport terminal was designed by architect Eero Saarinen. Photo courtesy of Metropolitan Washington Airports Authority.

Washington Dulles was conceived, designed, and built to meet the needs of a growing regional economy, and today it is a cornerstone of that growth. The U.S. Congress authorized a new airport in the 1950s, choosing famed architect Eero Saarinen as its designer. Saarinen soon realized his vision of an airport that would capture the soul of flight. Built on 10,000 acres of Virginia farmland 26 miles west of Washington, the Washington Dulles International terminal building was selected for a First Honor Award by the American Institute of Architects.

Named for the late Secretary of State John Foster Dulles and dedicated by President John F. Kennedy in 1962, Washington Dulles has kept pace with rapid growth. It is a symbol of progress for the more than 45,000 passengers who pass through it each day—nearly 20 million a year. Dulles is one of the fastest growing airports in the world.

As the global gateway for the nation's capital, Loudoun County and the rest of Northern Virginia, Dulles's international carriers connect 28 markets and bring 3.3 million international passengers through the facility. Dulles provides daily nonstop flights to 74 U.S. cities. General aviation—private and corporate aircraft so important to the area's business sector—serves more than 80,000 passengers yearly. Dulles is also meeting higher demands for cargo shipments, achieving a record volume of 783 million pounds in 1998.

Originally built to accommodate 6 million passengers per year, Dulles has undergone dramatic expansion, recently including new midfield concourses for regional and international flights. The extension of the original terminal in the late 1990s was done according to Saarinen's design.

State-of-the-art landing systems, Doppler radar, and enhanced runway systems give Washington Dulles an outstanding safety record. The airport also offers many amenities to the traveler—valet parking, shops with competitively priced merchandise in Dulles Marketplace, express meals at many of the airport's fine eateries, full accommodation for disabilities, foreign language assistance and currency exchange, and nearly 23,000 parking spaces.

The airport's economic contribution to the region is extraordinary. A pleasant 15-minute drive down the Greenway from Leesburg, Loudoun's county seat, the powerful presence of Dulles is a critical factor in attracting and retaining new business. It is directly responsible for more than 15,000 jobs, 30 percent of which are filled by Loudoun County residents. Indirect and visitor industry-related employment accounts for an additional 60,000 jobs, and Loudoun County reaps its fair share of these, as well. Airport activity generated $136 million in state and local taxes in 1998, while visitors using Dulles created another $277 million.

In 1986, Washington Dulles International and what is now Ronald Reagan Washington National Airport became part of the independent Metropolitan Washington Airports Authority. This committed organization ensures that the growing aviation needs of the region will be met by our world-class airports.

The future of Dulles Airport is seen in the new Concourse B, which provides spacious facilities and a variety of eateries and shops. Photo courtesy of Metropolitan Washington Airports Authority.

Blending Tradition With Innovation

Loudoun County Transportation Association

As the state's designated public transit provider, Loudoun County Transportation Association offers a coordinated, efficient system of broadly accessible public transportation to all residents. A not-for-profit organization, LCTA applies to the county's Board of Supervisors for funding each year and makes quarterly reports on its growing operations. Its volunteer board of directors comprises leaders from the county, its towns, and commercial sector. Loudoun Transit enjoys the full support of the community, and is a member of the United Way.

Within Loudoun County, a fleet of 19 ADA-compliant buses travel fixed routes and respond to calls for curb-to-curb service. The routes cover the entire county. In addition to local routes, there are daily connectors to Reston, to MARC trains in nearby Brunswick via Lovettsville, and to the Vienna Metro station—the western terminus of Washington, D.C.'s subway system. Loudoun Transit is Leesburg's contract ticket agent for Greyhound and operates its station, offering seamless connections for residents with distant travel plans.

"The system is not promoted as an alternative for the individual commuter," says a Loudoun Transit spokesman. "Our most frequent riders are senior citizens, the economically disadvantaged, or the physically handicapped who need transportation for health care, shopping, and other basic needs." True to its mission, Loudoun Transit will not deny rides to persons facing an immediate crisis.

Loudoun Transit supports the growing local economy in a number of innovative ways. In addition to shuttling airline industry workers to and from Dulles, it also transports groups who fly here to attend several training centers in the area. For workers in Washington's immediate Northern Virginia suburbs who increasingly find work in Loudoun County, its buses meet those "reverse commute" needs.

Seventy-five percent of Loudoun Transit's funding comes from federal, state, and local dollars, and public-private partnerships account for much of the remaining 25 percent—a win-win arrangement for all. These partnerships include retail outlets and the Loudoun Hospital Center, which provide funding for hourly service. The arrangement contributes to the viability of these businesses while ensuring access to those who need the services.

Similar arrangements are available for corporations relocating to Loudoun, and complement the efforts of the county's Department of Economic Development. "For what it costs businesses to pave their parking spaces, this entire system can be funded for one year," says the transit director. "We can custom design a plan to meet the customer's needs and move workers where they need to be—even if it involves several counties." Such plans have a positive environmental impact, as well.

LCTA provided nearly 80,000 one-way rides in 1999 alone, and ridership shows remarkable growth each year. The creation of Loudoun Transit's new headquarters, now under way, will meet expanding transportation needs. This visionary nonprofit is one of the reasons that Loudoun County is on the move. ◢

Within Loudoun County, a fleet of 19 ADA-compliant buses travel fixed routes and respond to calls for curb-to-curb service. Photo by Photoworks.

Loudoun Transit is Leesburg's contract ticket agent for Greyhound and operates its station, offering seamless connections for residents with distant travel plans. Photo by Photoworks.

Loudoun

WAGE, AM 1200

WAGE remote broadcasts take place throughout Loudoun County.

WAGE, AM 1200 is Loudoun County's one and only radio station. It went on the air in 1958 as a small sunup-to-sundown station in Leesburg. It has grown with the county to be a 24-hour, full-service radio station dedicated to giving residents of Loudoun County their first daily national, regional, and local news, traffic, and weather. Traveling Loudouners can keep up-to-date with all the news from home at WAGE.com.

It is the first place in the morning Loudouners can learn about local school closings during inclement weather. It is the only station to broadcast Loudoun County high school football games. It is the flagship station for George Washington University basketball. It's the only station in northern Virginia to carry Virginia Tech football. And Loudouners can hear their beloved Washington Redskins live on WAGE each Sunday from September to at least December.

WAGE begins its live broadcast day with world news from the USA radio network. As commuters drive to work they receive weather and traffic updates both inside and outside the beltway from Metro Traffic Control. If there was a county Board of Supervisors meeting, town council, or school board meeting the night before, WAGE news has a summary of whatever transpired on its early morning local newscasts.

WAGE's format has changed over the years. At various times it has played adult contemporary and country music. Now, in recognition of the fact that the FM band produces higher fidelity sound, WAGE, which broadcasts on the AM band, operates as an all-service station. Its primary mission —in the absence of daily local newspapers—is to be the information Voice of the Dulles Technological Corridor. It aims to supply the news of the region; broadcast sports of the area which cannot be heard elsewhere; and inform with a variety of talk shows that range from the national psychologist Dr. Joy Browne and financial experts The Dolans, to local Reston psychologist Dr. Sally Horwatt.

Since it went on the air more than 40 years ago, WAGE has garnered many awards from United Press International, the Virginia Association of Broadcasters, and the National Association of Broadcasters. It is a past winner of the NAB's prestigious Crystal Award for distinguished public service broadcasting. It has been a three-time finalist in the '90s for the National Association of Broadcasters' Marconi Award as Small Market Station of the year. UPI and VNN have both recognized WAGE repeatedly for its outstanding local news coverage. Most recently the Loudoun County Chamber of Commerce honored WAGE as the county's Small Business of the Year.

WAGE isn't the biggest station in the Washington metropolitan area, but it has an enviable record of training young talents who subsequently go on to radio and TV stations in large markets. It has always been the station's philosophy to give gifted but inexperienced young broadcasters an opportunity they would be unable to receive in big-city stations. In return, listeners benefit from their enthusiasm and creativity. The result is that Loudouners hear big-time radio from their small-town station, and that makes WAGE the Sound Choice for listeners in Loudoun County.

WAGE's live on-location broadcasts generate excitement and enthusiasm at local business and community events.

Blending Tradition With Innovation

Photo by David Galen.

Loudoun

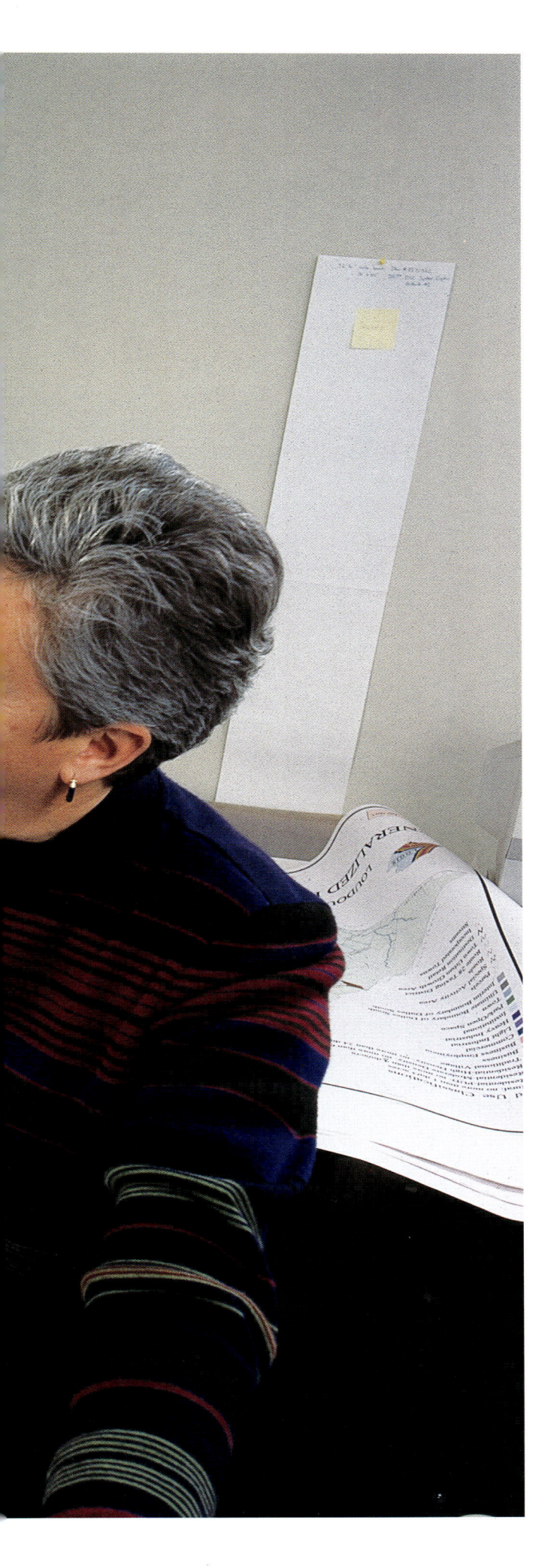

Blending Tradition With Innovation

Chapter Eleven

Professions and Building Loudoun County

Merrill Lynch, 96-97
The Miles/LeHane Group, Inc., 98-99
Talbot and Company, Inc., 100-101
Sevila, Saunders, Huddleston & White, 102
Galen Photography, 103

From money management to architecture, Loudoun firms are recognized as leaders in their fields. Photo by David Galen.

Merrill Lynch

When Merrill Lynch opened its financial management office in 1996, it introduced a new corporate vision to Loudoun County. The undisputed leader in planning-based financial advice and management, Merrill Lynch provides personal, technology-enhanced relationships with its hallmark global footprint.

Merrill Lynch partners (left to right) John Sheehan and Patrick Huge are committed to helping Loudoun County citizens manage their economic health.

Offering securities underwriting, trading and brokering, trust services, personal financial planning, investment banking, research, personal credit, and insurance, Merrill Lynch's client interactions are built on the model of private banking relationships. In a technology-focused market where the phenomenon of the day trader has made its mark, Merrill Lynch holds to the belief that real customer value is in combining technology with human expertise and wisdom, creating collaborations that are based on relationships and focused on the long term.

Located in Leesburg and managing significant Loudoun assets, this Merrill Lynch branch office has built its healthy client base through referrals from other satisfied clients. The firm offers individuals and institutions the resources of Merrill Lynch's worldwide assets. It also offers the local networks and individual attention of local financial consultants who manage relationships, not just portfolios. Although individual clients comprise nearly 70 percent of the business at the end of 1999, Loudoun's robust economic environment is stimulating an increasing share of the corporate and institutional market.

For people seeking knowledgeable assistance with any facet of personal finances, be it property transactions, estate planning, structuring insurance, or cash management, Merrill Lynch is ready to assist in every financial decision. Avoiding cookie-cutter client relationships, Merrill Lynch professionals consider each decision with the client's goals and dreams in mind. There are programs that encompass client choices and expert counsel for every portfolio size.

Their services include full financial analysis, on-line access, e-commerce, an unlimited number of accounts and trades, and many extras. This bold plan demands a trusting professional relationship—a role the staff at the Merrill Lynch Leesburg office accepts and enjoys.

"We're not stockbrokers; we are our customers' private CFO," says Patrick Huge. "We also act as the liaison with accountants, attorneys, and other professionals who work on our clients' behalf, creating a valuable private banking relationship."

Corporate and institutional clients, from family foundations to burgeoning high-tech businesses, benefit from the same personal attention and choices on a larger scale. Small businesses and employee benefit plans receive advice, guidance, and comprehensive strategic services that include liability and transition management and succession planning. Because of Merrill Lynch's assets and presence in 43 countries, it brings global expertise to local and international mergers and acquisitions. It held the top spot in global combined debt and equity underwriting during much of 1999.

As the county grows, and as traditionally rural parcels attract developers and multimillion-dollar capital gains, the firm is uniquely positioned to provide sound advice. Because of their established local network, all staff members can confidently refer clients to other resources, when necessary.

John Sheehan is the 1999 chairman of Loudoun County Chamber of Commerce's Board of Directors, and he also serves on the Waterford Foundation, which maintains a unique piece of Loudoun County history. Patrick Huge was appointed to the Loudoun County Historic District Review Committee and is a trustee of Loudoun Country Day School, the county's oldest private school. Both are fully involved in their community and in youth sports.

On the corporate level, Merrill Lynch has an impressive charitable network. The Merrill Lynch

Blending Tradition With Innovation

& Co. Foundation supports many educational institutions and initiatives, as well as health programs, cultural endeavors, and hundreds of community organizations in which its employees play active roles. It also carefully considers societal issues in its program design, one of which assists with the financial challenges facing nearly 15 million Americans who cope with severe disabilities.

How is Merrill Lynch faring in a changing industry? Through its wholly owned subsidiaries, Merrill Lynch is one of the world's largest asset managers. Farsighted investing balances current returns with future growth. While aggressively broadening its product line, it recorded record profits during the first half of 1999; the funds comprising more than half of its total fund-family assets outperformed the S&P 500. With the boom in e-trading, a 1999 Forrester PowerRankings consumer survey ranked client satisfaction for Merrill Lynch on-line services far higher than the proliferating dot-com start-ups.

According to Thomson Financial's First Call Corp., Merrill Lynch produced the most widely read research reports of any Wall Street firm. Its Global Research group became the first research organization to be ranked among the top five in six global surveys by *Institutional Investor*. Merrill Lynch won the *Wall Street Journal's* 1999 All-Star Analysts research survey, the third year in a row for this honor. And United Kingdom-based *Global Finance* magazine gave Merrill Lynch a triple honor: Best Bank in North America for Research, Best Bank in Asia for Equity Origination, and Best Global Management Bank.

The partners at Merrill Lynch's Leesburg office say the firm is committed to staying in Loudoun County and helping citizens manage their economic health. There is no reason to expect a change in approach: "We're going to keep doing what we're doing well."

In a technology-focused market where the phenomenon of the day trader has made its mark, Merrill Lynch holds to the belief that real customer value is in combining technology with human expertise and wisdom, creating collaborations that are based on relationships and focused on the long term.

When Merrill Lynch opened its financial management office in 1996, it introduced a new corporate vision to Loudoun County.

97

The Miles/LeHane Group, Inc.

When David Miles acquired the business of his friend and mentor Lou LeHane, he had a keen understanding of the work he needed to do. LeHane was one of the founders of a new industry that assists senior level executives to change or enhance their career, and as LeHane's failing health forced him to seek a buyer for the business, Miles was himself at a career crossroads.

Today, the Miles/LeHane Group is achieving the vision of both men—to be a highly respected, specialized provider of custom career management and human resource development services to selected clients worldwide. Miles/LeHane offers full-service, cutting-edge solutions to problems faced by today's executives and their employers: mergers and acquisitions, downsizing, shifting expectations, new management paradigms, and professional burnout. Its clients range from Fortune 500 companies through small, rapidly growing high-tech firms, and include associations and other nonprofit organizations.

Miles/LeHane's principals have more than 100 years of combined experience in the executive workforce of the world's best known service organizations. The group focused on outplacement services during the struggling economy of the early '90s, and still boasts a 100-percent placement rate. Miles/LeHane has since diversified to enhance the executive's value through coaching for leadership, performance, and development. Consulting and training are available to corporate customers who can benefit from this knowledgeable group's skills for training programs, needs assessments, and the full scope of human resource services. Miles/LeHane's business alliance with the Whyte Group, Inc., a national search firm, has positioned it for growth in the executive search field.

Founded in 1978 as LeHane Consulting, David Miles took the helm in 1992. As the director of human resource development for Marriott Corporation's 130,000 employees in contract services, his involvement in its restructuring and downsizing and his doctorate studies in human resource development readied him for new possibilities.

The story of Miles/LeHane is intertwined with the marvelous structure it calls home, the Glenfiddich House in Leesburg. The Civil War-era mansion had been used as a rooming house and had fallen into disrepair, even though former boarders included author James Dickey, who penned *Deliverance* in a small back bedroom. After a fire in 1979, the house was slated for demolition but was saved by Lou LeHane as a possible office location.

Recovered diaries proved that his inclinations were correct: General Robert E. Lee used the house to recover from injuries before heading north to the bloody Battle of Antietam. With Traveller stabled in the back, he met there with Stonewall Jackson and Jeb Stuart, and from its library, watched his son Bob leave him for the last time through the still-prominent rows of boxwoods; Bob Lee was captured in battle.

The LeHanes, and later David Miles and his partner in business and in life, Melanie, filled the home with priceless antiques. The painstaking restoration and maintenance of Glenfiddich House has enriched the whole community; the group opens the home to Leesburg for historical tours and charitable events, returning the once-doomed site to the town as a local treasure.

Headquartered in the historic district of Loudoun County's largest town—Leesburg, Virginia—Glenfiddich House is an hour's drive from Washington, D.C. Photo by David Galen.

A relaxed, informal atmosphere prevails in this antebellum home which General Robert E. Lee frequented and where author James Dickey wrote Deliverance. *Photo by David Galen.*

Blending Tradition With Innovation

Most important, Glenfiddich House provides a uniquely impressive environment for Miles/LeHane's innovative in-residence program, where executives needing outplacement assistance find help available 24 hours a day—and go to sleep in General Lee's bedroom at night. Clients arrive at Glenfiddich House almost immediately after losing their job. They spend three to five days with a counselor who deals with all aspects of the loss and presents the tools for effective career transition. When clients leave, they are ready to succeed.

The Miles/LeHane Group displays good citizenship. It has received Loudoun County's Business of the Year Award (for small service businesses) and was one of two top fund-raisers for the area's Muscular Dystrophy drive. In November 1998, the group and its innovative approaches were featured on the CBS program *Eye on Business* and in September 1999 on ABC's *Business Now*. David Miles stays at the leading edge of his industry, serving as president of the International Board of Career Management Certification.

"Loudoun County is a good place for this kind of enterprise, and I believe that we are good for Loudoun County," says Miles. As a commercial organization that imposes little burden on Loudoun's environment, Miles/LeHane nevertheless exposes the county and the town of Leesburg to increasing numbers of influential business people.

The group's future reflects the success of northern Virginia's business community. With additional offices now in Winchester, Virginia; Bethesda, Maryland; and Washington, D.C., David Miles forecasts continued expansion of the firm's human resources services. As Loudoun County continues to grow, Miles sees a more active role in the healthy local employment market.

"We must be more responsive to the demands of a global economy, where action is expected 24 hours a day, 7 days a week, 365 days a year," says Miles. "Some businesses may not know how to add value to the organization through nontraditional jobs, which may be off-site, flexibly scheduled, or contracted. But it's often the key to customer service. We're talking about new ways of doing business."

"Working 25 years for a company and receiving your gold watch is not the model for today," Miles continues. "Changing jobs was seen as a mark of disloyalty. Today, the loyalty we foster is to the profession—to making sure that the skill base is the best it can be, and that it is marketable."

Loudoun County offers an example of the challenges that businesses must address. It includes a still-rural environment in the west and a booming high-tech world in the east. "These companies will be employing workers from the western area," says Miles, "but they don't always know how to effectively communicate. We can be the bridge builder."

Change is happening; to stand still is to be left behind. Miles/LeHane provides the dialogue for seizing the opportunities of change and navigating them productively.

The mansion's formal living room is a comfortable setting for consulting with clients or receiving guests. Photo by David Galen.

David Miles, chairman, and Melanie Miles, vice president and chief operating officer, host many executive meetings throughout the year in the mansion's formal dining room. Photo by David Galen.

Loudoun

Talbot and Company, Inc.

When Helena Scott Talbot, broker, founded her real estate firm in 1995, she brought together a love of Loudoun County with a commitment to having her company on the cutting edge of technology. With 20 years of real estate experience in Loudoun, Helena also drew upon the expertise of her husband and partner, John Talbot. John is a respected realtor with a 45-year history of both listing and selling estate properties, primarily in the Middleburg area. Today, Talbot and Company, Inc. is comprised of 11 full-time agents and 12 referral agents. All professionals are from diverse backgrounds and are able to meet the entire spectrum of Loudoun's real estate needs.

Talbot and Company, with an office in Leesburg's historic district, works with both buyers and sellers in the fast-paced Loudoun real estate market. The Talbot team is committed to using state-of-the-art technology in order to achieve the best possible results for its clients. With the company's two real estate web sites, sellers discover that their home is exposed throughout the world to the most buyers, while buyers find they are able to shop for real estate on their own time. The Talbot team of professionals listens to the needs of its clients and, in utilizing its technological resources, is able to help clients smoothly and successfully navigate their way through a real estate transaction. Since real estate is generally the single most important investment most people make in their lifetime, the Talbot professionals take the responsibility of their clients very seriously. According to Helena, the goal of Talbot and Company is to not only help their clients buy and sell real estate but also to make their clients so happy with the process that they come back again and again.

Nearly all Talbot agents have earned the Accredited Buyer Representative designation enabling them to work exclusively in their buyers' best interest. Talbot agents are well-versed on helping their clients with qualifying for loans and in helping them locate the most favorable interest rates. Buyers get priority access to no money down and no closing cost loans or low down payment loans with great interest rates. As a free service, clients who plan a home purchase can submit their desired home or land profile and receive first notice of all properties new to the market. In a competitive real estate market, this means that Talbot and Company buyers have an instant advantage over others seeking similar properties.

For Loudoun's home sellers, the Talbot and Company professionals produce surefire results to get their property sold with proven techniques tailored towards an individualized marketing strategy. Buyers are qualified before a property is shown so that the offer to purchase moves swiftly. Settlements proceed smoothly because the Talbot professionals keep their clients fully informed every step of the way. Free relocation services help satisfied sellers find property anywhere in the United States.

The Talbot team of professionals holds memberships in the National and Virginia Association of

The Talbot teams consists of (front row, left to right) Karen Jones, Helena Talbot, Mary Pelot, (back row) Chuck Jones, Sharon Bankhead, Gilda Montel, Robert Allison, Phyllis Allen, David Ulrich, Tan Tunador, (not pictured) John Talbot, Della Bogaty, Jeff Curtis, and Bruce Allen. Photo by Howard O. Allen.

The Loudoun County land specialists make technology work for their clients. Photo by Howard O. Allen.

Blending Tradition With Innovation

The Talbot team has a deep appreciation for Loudoun's historic properties. Photo by Howard O. Allen.

Realtors, the Real Estate Buyers Agent Council, the Real Estate Brokers Management Council, the Realtor's Land Institute, and the National Trust for Historic Preservation. Reflecting their regional focus, they are members of the Dulles Area Association of Realtors, where Helena has served as a director.

Talbot and Company knows that a healthy real estate market reflects a desirable quality of life in Loudoun County. Its agents are committed to preserving the character of Loudoun. The Talbot agents believe in supporting their community, and various members of the team serve on the Leesburg Economic Development Commission, the Friends of the Thomas Balch Library, the Loudoun Tourism Council, the Loudoun County Chamber of Commerce, the County's Open Space Advisory Committee, and its Rural Economic Development Task Force.

Talbot and Company's real estate professionals come from backgrounds in banking, finance, international relations, corporate marketing, teaching, and hotel management. With multilingual capabilities in French, Spanish, and Turkish and a respect for local traditions, the Talbot team can comfortably relate to international business executives as well as native Loudoun residents. Sellers know that Talbot and Company will not only protect their interests but also the best interests of the total Loudoun environment.

Talbot and Company primarily specializes in the selling of Loudoun County's homes, farms, estates, and land west of the Route 15 corridor. Several of its agents, however, specialize in the hot market of eastern Loudoun's planned communities. Not only do Helena and her agents conduct business in Loudoun County, but they also live the Loudoun lifestyle and understand its changes.

Helena learned to love the county as a child when she summered in Paconian Springs with her grandparents. She returned to live permanently in Loudoun in 1976 and to raise her two children, Alex and Samantha. Samantha is carrying on the family real estate tradition by working for a new home builder. Her husband, Tan, is a realtor with Talbot and Company and is consistently a top producing agent. You can often see Helena on her daily long-distance jogs on back country roads. Watch for Helena and John touring the county's many picturesque byways on their Harley Davidson motorcycles—Helena on her Springer and John on his custom Softtail.

Talbot and Company offers world-class service to Loudoun's discriminating buyers and sellers. "Our first priority is not volume," says Helena, "but rather striving for unparalleled individual service and long-term relationships." Continuing education, a positive attitude, a high work ethic, and integrity keep Helena Scott Talbot and her agents on the leading edge of real estate service for their clients. ◾

Helena and John Talbot tour Loudoun's countryside on their Harley Davidson motorcycles. Photo by Howard O. Allen.

Sevila, Saunders, Huddleston & White

Sevila, Saunders, Huddleston & White is located near the County Court complex in Leesburg and borrows a traditional Virginia ambiance from its historic district setting. The firm handles all aspects of corporate, personal, family, and civil practice, as well as misdemeanor and felony criminal defense. Photo by The Art of Photography.

Sevila, Saunders, Huddleston & White, P.C. is one of Loudoun County's oldest law firms. Attorneys leading the firm include (standing left to right) Jon D. Huddleston, Craig E. White, Jeanine M. Irving, Jeffrey A. Tuten, (seated left to right) Robert E. Sevila, and Richard R. Saunders. Photo by The Art of Photography.

Sevila, Saunders, Huddleston & White, P.C. is one of Loudoun County's oldest law firms and traces its roots back to 1929. A general practice firm, it handles all aspects of corporate, personal, family, and civil practice, as well as misdemeanor and felony criminal defense. It is located near the County Court complex in Leesburg and borrows a traditional Virginia ambiance from its historic district setting.

Because law is increasingly complex and pervasive, Sevila, Saunders, Huddleston & White helps citizens exercise their rights and understand their responsibilities in consumer, employment, property, and estate cases—wherever law impacts their lives. The firm also represents prominent northern Virginia businesses and utility companies, and often serves as Special Counsel to area county and municipal governments.

The practice addresses the needs of both old and new Loudoun County, and relationships are a priority. "We worked for the parents, and now we are working for the next generation," says one partner. Sevila, Saunders, Huddleston & White believes that its years of service in the community make a difference, and the firm's reputation reflects that belief.

Robert E. Sevila served as mayor for the Town of Leesburg from 1982 to 1992, and is on the teaching faculty at a nearby university. He is vice president of the Loudoun County Chamber of Commerce and chairman-elect for 2002. Sevila is also a cofounder of the Bank of Potomac (now F&M Bank-Northern Virginia) and a charter member of its board of directors.

Richard Saunders has served as a member of the Ethics Committee of the Virginia State Bar, and both Saunders and Sevila are past presidents of the Loudoun County Bar Association. Jon Huddleston has held leadership roles in the Young Lawyers Conference and the Conference of Local Bar Associations and is a member of the faculty of the Virginia State Bar Professionalism Course. Craig White has served as an officer and director of the Loudoun County Bar and is a member of the Family Law Section of the Virginia State Bar. Associates Jeff Tuten and Jeanine Irving continue the firm's tradition of leadership. All attorneys are active in numerous professional organizations.

The firm consistently receives the highest rating for its professional and ethical standards—the AV rating—from Martindale-Hubbell, the leading guide to attorneys and law firms around the world. The partners are deservedly proud that former colleagues are now judges in various state courts, including the Virginia Supreme Court.

In addition to representing the interests of Loudoun's citizens, the attorneys of Sevila, Saunders, Huddleston & White share their expertise and time through a variety of local activities, including the YMCA, Little League baseball, Blue Ridge Speech and Hearing, American Heart Association, and the preservation of General George Marshall's home. "We believe in using our skills to help the community," says Bob Sevila.

"This is a gathering of friends," says one of the employees, who notes that the group enjoys working together and serving others. The staff is loyal; most of the employees have been with the firm for 15 years or more, and they have developed close working relationships with many of the firm's clients. Notwithstanding the rapid growth of Loudoun County and inevitable expansion of the firm, the attorneys and staff are committed to maintaining their personal association with their clients, old and new.

Blending Tradition With Innovation

Galen Photography

Photography has been David Galen's lifelong avocation, and in 1991 he made it his business. The former corporate analyst's management skills, technical knowledge, and creativity equipped him for success; now his company is a full-service commercial imaging business with an impressive track record in Loudoun County.

Galen started his business by photographing special events for associations. With a keen eye for architecture, landscapes, and pictures that tell a story, Galen's advertising and corporate image photographs soon drew attention. Now his work is used in a broad range of marketing publications, trade show exhibits, Internet sites, and computer-based training modules.

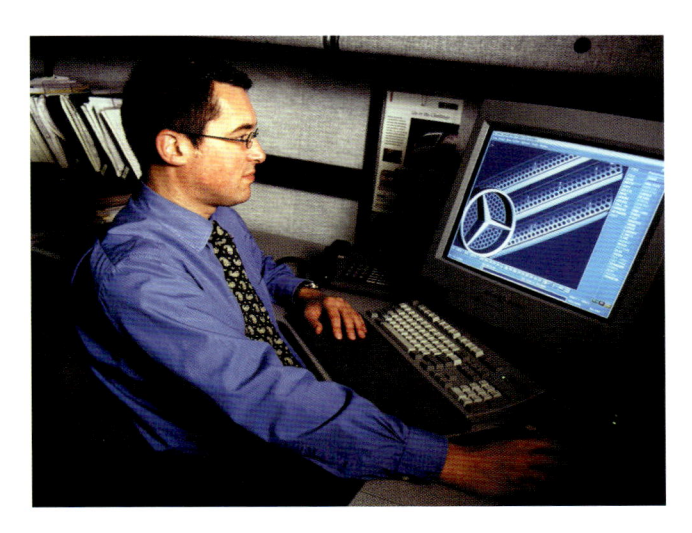

David Galen's lens has focused on Loudoun County since 1994. His distinctive photographs promoting a thriving community in which to live, work, and play are used by the Loudoun Tourism Council, the county's Department of Economic Development, the Town of Leesburg, and the Chamber of Commerce. Galen's images on the Chamber's 2000 directory cover evoke Loudoun's evolution from an agrarian county to a high-tech corporate center. AIRBUS, United Airlines, Loudoun Healthcare, and REHAU, Inc. are a few of Galen's corporate clients in Loudoun County.

David Galen believes that every organization has a story to tell. Working closely with his clients, Galen crafts a customer value message that can be visualized through his photographic images. He often works with art directors, graphic designers, illustrators, and printers to create innovative presentations for corporate annual reports, promotional brochures, and web sites. The product may also be an educational tool that impacts quality of life—shock-trauma centers nationwide feature the Brain Injury Resource Center, a touch screen computer kiosk that answers questions about spinal cord injuries using images created by Galen Photography.

David Galen serves on the board of directors of the Loudoun County Chamber of Commerce and the Committee for Dulles, is chairman of the Loudoun Buyers Exchange, and president of PHOTOFORUM, a professional roundtable that addresses business and technical issues within the industry. In 1996, Galen Photography was nominated for the county's Service Business of the Year award.

His customers are more than satisfied. "His image of the surgery suite . . . was the key to winning the Associated Builders and Contractors Excellence in Construction Award," says a spokesperson for Scott Long Construction. A MICROS Systems, Inc. manager notes that "David Galen has created hundreds of photos for use in our print and on-line productions. He is at his best when acting as a contributor to the creative process and . . . gets to the idea behind the photo."

At Galen Photography, assignments are successful when clients see their messages conveyed with imagination and integrity. "Your image," says David Galen, "is our only business."

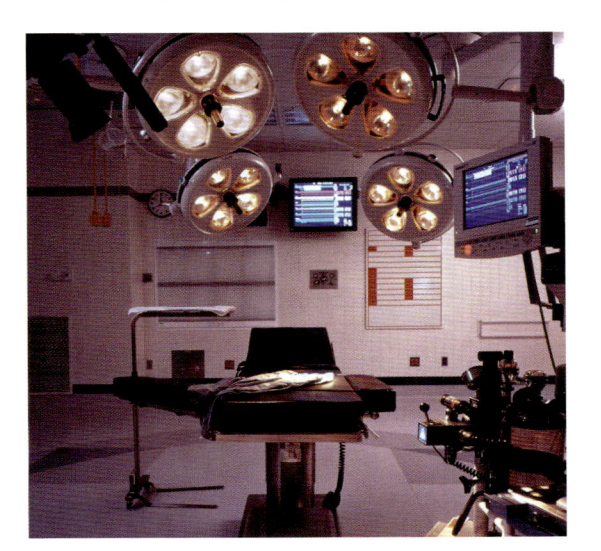

(above) With a keen eye for architecture, landscapes, and pictures that tell a story, Galen's advertising and corporate image photographs soon drew attention.

(left) Galen's work is used in a broad range of marketing publications, trade show exhibits, Internet sites, and computer-based training modules.

(left) Working closely with his clients, Galen crafts a customer value message that can be visualized through his photographic images.

103

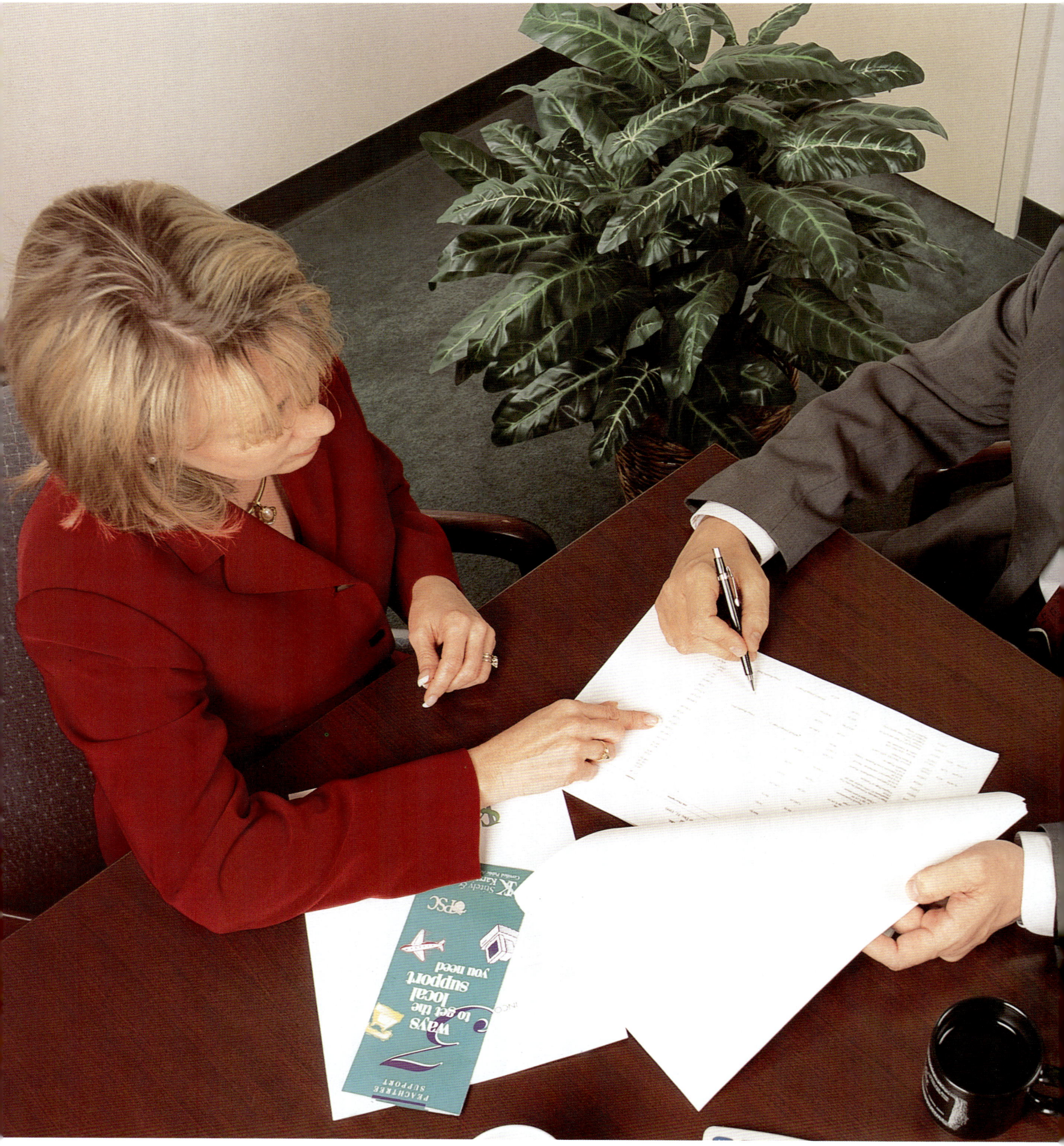

Blending Tradition With Innovation

Chapter Twelve
Business and Finance

The Town of Leesburg, Virginia, 106-109
Loudoun County Chamber of Commerce, 110-111
Loudoun County Government, 112-113

Loudoun County's government entities and the Chamber of Commerce offer a strong base for the area's growing economy. Photo by David Galen.

Loudoun

The Town of Leesburg, Virginia

Leesburg is a success story at the crossroads of yesterday and tomorrow. It is a place where the old is cherished and the new is welcomed, neither at the expense of the other. From the historic Potomac River through the quaint brick-and-stone downtown to the busy bypass and malls on its growing edge, Leesburg gracefully displays its fine Virginia heritage. The town's convenient location makes it easy to visit for the day, the weekend, or the week: it is just a 15-minute drive from world-class Washington Dulles International Airport or a 5-minute drive from the 15-car White's Ferry across the Potomac River.

Originally named "George Town" after England's reigning monarch, this green and rolling land belonging to Lord Fairfax was at the intersection of two important colonial roads. Fairfax's surveyor, John Hough, mapped and subdivided 60 acres of land for Colonel Nicholas Minor of the Virginia Militia in 1757. An act of the Assembly in the colonial capital of Williamsburg formally established the Town of Leesburg in 1758, honoring the commonwealth's remarkable Lee family. The Lees of Virginia would later include a signer of the Declaration of Independence and General Robert E. Lee.

As the county seat of Loudoun, Leesburg quickly developed as a center of government, trading, and commerce for the area east of the Blue Ridge Mountains. Tradesmen and innkeepers set up shops to serve the lawyers and politicians who came to town on official business. In the mid-1800s, a rail line planned from the Alexandria seaport to the Virginia frontier—now West Virginia—passed through town, although it never quite made it over the mountains. Nevertheless, the railroad permanently tied Leesburg to Washington, D.C., and the towns between.

Strategically located, Leesburg is forever linked to the nation's early military history. The British army used the town as a staging ground during the French and Indian War, and the colonial militia established a supply area there during the American Revolution. When the British besieged Washington during the War of 1812, patriots smuggled America's most treasured documents, including the Constitution and the Declaration of Independence, to Leesburg for safekeeping. The town also played a prominent role during the Civil War. Ball's Bluff National Cemetery stands at the strategic point where rebel troops pushed the Yankees back across the Potomac River. General Robert E. Lee recovered from injuries in Leesburg before pushing ahead to the fateful Maryland Campaign. Authentic reenactments of nearby Civil War battles draw many military history enthusiasts to the region.

Leesburg, however, is more than just a fascinating place to visit. It also represents small town living at its best. The town is a beautiful place to live and a rewarding place to do business. With its low unemployment and carefully planned growth, this historic town offers families a chance to attain the American dream. Schools, parks, and shopping easily accommodate Leesburg's rapidly growing population. Recreation leagues provide opportunities for young and old alike. The town's largest park, Ida Lee Park, includes a comprehensive recreation center with an indoor pool, gymnasium, and fitness room. The town also offers a number of housing choices—residents can invest in an older home and own a piece of history, or they can choose to join the growing planned communities on the town's perimeter.

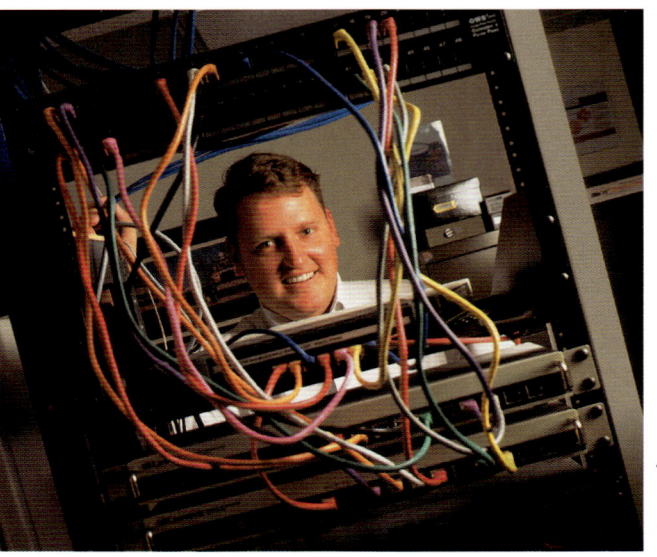

Historic reenactments and special events are part of the fabric of the Leesburg community.

Young entrepreneurs have found Leesburg to be a hotbed for high-tech business.

Blending Tradition With Innovation

Quality of life issues are important to Leesburg. It is a town where family values represent more than just an overused expression. Its religious institutions have played, and continue to play, a significant role in the life of the community. While Loudoun County is building many new schools to accommodate the growth in its eastern region, the town's schools are well established and offer a wealth of extracurricular and sport activities that garner enthusiastic support from residents. Two local newspapers and a radio station keep residents up-to-date on local events and offer the hometown perspective to the national news being made just down the Potomac.

In addition to its many recreational facilities and competitive housing market, the town's tax rate is ranked one of the lowest in the Washington area and supports a smoothly run system of town services. An elected seven-member council, including the mayor, governs the town. Leesburg has a government with a personal touch and makes service to the town's citizens a priority. The town's law enforcement is based on community policing, and most neighborhoods know their officer's name. The Town Government Center is a modern facility that blends seamlessly with its neighboring historic buildings.

The town is the hub of the county and offers businesses and residents an established and stable infrastructure. Its reliable, yet environmentally sensitive, water and sewer system replaces 99 percent of the aquifer to the same Potomac River watershed that supplies it. Town leaders boast that Leesburg's streets are cleared of winter snows before many of the surrounding jurisdictions.

The heart of Leesburg is its historic district, part of the National Register of America's treasures. It offers one of the best preserved and most picturesque historic downtowns in Virginia, where period interpreters enhance the well-documented walking tour of 50 historic sites. Many houses along King Street served as hospitals to the Civil War wounded, including future Supreme Court Justice Oliver Wendell Holmes. The city's leaders can confidently say that downtown will look the same many years from now, thanks to careful zoning and planning. When the sun sets behind the Blue Ridge Mountains and casts a glow across Leesburg's quaint, tree-lined streets, there is no lovelier place to be.

Among its treasures are the Loudoun Museum and the Thomas Balch Library, where genealogists can scan census records for the entire Commonwealth. Scholars can examine deeds, wills, cemetery and marriage records, archival diaries, and maps dating back to pre-Revolutionary times, as well as an outstanding Civil War collection. The courthouse in Leesburg maintains land records from 1757 to the present.

Historic landmarks and stately mansions that are open to the public flank the town. President James Monroe wrote his famous Monroe Doctrine at his Oak Hill plantation, just south of town. Also to the south is Oatlands, built in 1803 from bricks molded and fired on the property. Its well-attended events include antiques fairs and productions in its Carriage Theatre. Morven Park, at the town's west end, is a 1,200-acre estate that served as the home to

Families flock to the Washington and Old Dominion Trail, a former railroad line converted to a 45-mile walking and biking trail that passes through Leesburg.

The Loudoun Museum's gift shop is housed in one of the town's oldest buildings, a former silversmith shop dating from 1767.

Loudoun

World War II chief of staff and postwar statesman, General George C. Marshall hosted many prominent visitors at his Leesburg home, Dodona Manor.

governors of both Maryland and Virginia. Known for its gardens, Carriage Museum, and its Museum of Hounds and Hunting, the estate is part of the rich imagery of Virginia's piedmont.

Among those who have called Leesburg home is General George C. Marshall, who retired to his beloved Dodona Manor after World War II. It was from Dodona, within the historic district, that President Harry Truman called Marshall back into the service of his country to become the architect of economic recovery for postwar Europe—the Marshall Plan. Author-humorist Russell Baker, who chronicled his Loudoun County childhood in the best-selling *Growing Up*, lives in the historic district. Radio and television entertainer Arthur Godfrey made enormous contributions to his hometown, and the town's municipal airport is named to honor him.

The Leesburg Executive Airport, known as Godfrey Field, is just a short ride up the Greenway from Dulles International Airport. This airport, location of Piedmont Hawthorne Aviation, welcomes a growing number of private and corporate aircraft and offers training, rentals, and charters. Leesburg's aviation focus includes the Federal Aviation Administration's Dulles Air Route Traffic Control Center, one of the county's largest employers. The international firm REHAU, Inc. chose Leesburg as its corporate headquarters partly because of nearby equestrian opportunities—there are many reasons to do business in Leesburg.

A thriving regional economy and the influx of high-tech industries to Loudoun County have brought Leesburg to the attention of large corporations and small entrepreneurial enterprises. The town attracts business not only because it is a player in the booming Northern Virginia economy, but also because it is a crucial 10 miles from the hustle of high-density development and commerce. It reaps the benefits of both proximity and distance.

Leesburg offers an enticing assortment of retail enterprises for the shopper, making it a popular destination for day trips from the nation's capital, as well as a service-oriented town for its residents. An antique enthusiast's dream, Leesburg's many quaint shops attract buyers from the entire East

The Federal Aviation Administration is one of Leesburg's largest employers.

Blending Tradition With Innovation

Coast. Market Station presents a fine example of a reclaimed industrial site for attractive shops, a tourist center, and dining. At Leesburg's growing eastern edge, the Premium Outlet Mall offers the best of brands and the best of bargains. More than 70 restaurants cater to a wide variety of tastes, and lodging options include the gracious Norris House and Laurel Brigade Inns. Within a county well served by the hospitality industry, nearby conference centers cater to Leesburg's business demands.

The town offers families and visitors the chance to participate in a variety of activities. Driving into town on Virginia's Route 7, a roadside sign announces upcoming community events. Whether it's the monthly First Friday Gallery Walk—when Leesburg's shops and galleries serve wine and cheese as they introduce new or well-known artists—the Celtic Festival, summer's outdoor Bluemont Concerts, or the Flower and Garden Show, there's always something to do. Leesburg also loves parades, and boasts the longest Halloween parade east of the Mississippi.

One of northern Virginia's favorite summer events takes place in Leesburg each year. August Court Days recreates the excitement of the town's eighteenth-century life, when court was in session and craftsmen plied their wares. Hundreds of colonial reenactors stage mock trials and offer a bounty of historically informed entertainment and refreshment. The booths of Appalachia's artisans are extraordinarily popular with the thousands of visitors who converge on Leesburg for this two-day event.

Started at the crossroads more than two centuries ago, Leesburg is at a far busier crossroads today. Its leaders know that economic growth and development require a government that seeks the rewards while minimizing risks. Its plan for orderly growth and expansion has established, with citizen input, a deliberate process for preserving the Leesburg quality of life while taking advantage of the county's healthy economy. It is no small wonder that Leesburg is a model business location, a tourist destination, and a place that newcomers quickly call home. ◼

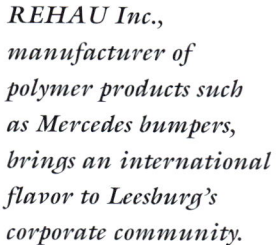

REHAU Inc., manufacturer of polymer products such as Mercedes bumpers, brings an international flavor to Leesburg's corporate community.

Leesburg Corner Premium Outlets, offering the country's top brand names, is a popular destination for residents and visitors alike.

109

Loudoun County Chamber of Commerce

The Loudoun County Chamber of Commerce is a leader in the region's amazing economic boom. With more than 1,200 members at the opening of the new century, the Chamber is the county's "voice of business," supporting thoughtful, sustained development of both new and existing enterprise. It is the second largest Chamber in the metropolitan Washington, D.C., area.

Merv Forney serves as the Loudoun County Chamber of Commerce Chairman of the Board for the year 2000. Photo by David Galen.

Formally organized in 1968, the Chamber's history reflects Loudoun County's evolution from an agricultural economy to a thriving business community. This growth, spurred by the opening of Washington Dulles International Airport in 1961, precipitated the creation of a united Loudoun Chamber that brought together several smaller Chamber organizations, some of which dated back to the Civil War. The Chamber's expansion owes much to the generous volunteer spirit of its members. Its active standing and special projects committees work with the Chamber's seven-person staff to provide services that strengthen both its membership and a community that is favorable to business expansion.

The Chamber facilitates networking through monthly Business Showcase Breakfasts that give members an opportunity to spotlight their enterprises, and evening mixers to provide a collegial atmosphere for building relationships. Photo by David Galen.

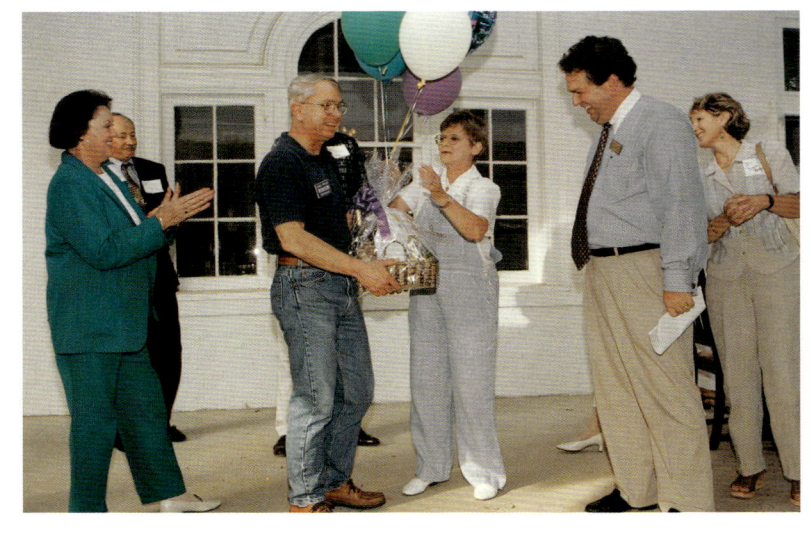

Loudoun County is unquestionably a giant in the technology and transportation industries, and the Loudoun County Chamber of Commerce counts corporate giants like America Online, MCI WorldCom, UUNET, PSI NET, Telos, Orbital Sciences, and United Airlines among its active members. But approximately three-quarters of the membership are small businesses with less than 10 employees, mirroring Loudoun's healthy entrepreneurial and agribusiness climate.

Chamber members get tremendous value for their dues dollar, and its *Membership Directory and Resource Guide* offers high visibility advertising opportunities. The Chamber facilitates networking through monthly Business Showcase Breakfasts that give members an opportunity to spotlight their enterprises, and evening mixers to provide a collegial atmosphere for building relationships. Leadshare and Buyers Exchange programs help grow businesses, and Small Business Expos and the annual Procurement Seminar enhance efficiency. The Chamber-sponsored Women's Expo provides a forum for career development and its related issues.

The Loudoun County Chamber of Commerce presents an annual trade show—Dulles Connection—that is its signature event, providing a popular and enjoyable opportunity for businesses to strengthen connections with each other and with regional consumers. An annual auction raises additional non-dues revenue for the Chamber.

As advocates for a probusiness public policy agenda, the Chamber publishes its legislative agenda to encourage area business leaders to make their voices heard. Chamber representatives regularly travel to Virginia's state capital in Richmond to support responsible business-friendly legislation, such as measures that enhance capital formation and investment opportunities. A strong proponent of revenue sharing, the Chamber is working to bring some of Loudoun's considerable state tax revenues back to the county for investment in transportation and schools. The Chamber also works closely with the Loudoun County Board of Supervisors and the seven town governments in the community.

Blending Tradition With Innovation

Recognizing that a skilled and available workforce is vital to the county's continued financial health, the Chamber presses for increased state funding for Virginia's colleges, universities, and noncredit technology training programs. In 1999, it aggressively supported a K-12 public school construction bond referendum to meet the needs of families who come to Loudoun for the excellent employment climate. The Chamber will continue to work with Loudoun's planners and the board of supervisors to ensure continued infrastructure development that matches the area's anticipated population growth.

The Chamber helps to inform Loudoun's citizens of the benefits of the county's position as an attractive home for business. As an advocate for environmentally clean county industry and for a careful balance between natural resource preservation and economic development, the Chamber takes an active role in the dialogue about Loudoun's land use. Food for Thought, the chamber's monthly educational lunch seminar, presents panels of Chamber members to address business issues of community interest and is open to the public.

An enhanced web site (www.loudounchamber.org) tells the Chamber's story and links visitors to additional programs that attract and serve business; the site's continuing development will reflect Loudoun's position as an Internet giant as it expands e-commerce and marketing for members. *Loudounclear*, the monthly chamber newsletter, highlights Chamber events and timely, valuable business information. An informal bimonthly electronic newsletter keeps members up-to-date on issues of common concern.

Chamber members are community leaders who take their responsibilities seriously. The Loudoun County Chamber of Commerce sponsors an annual charity golf tournament at the popular Raspberry Falls Golf and Hunt Club—an always sold-out event that, in 1999, raised more $20,000 for the Chamber and its designated local charities. Every other year, the Chamber honors Loudoun's fire, rescue, and law enforcement personnel with an event featuring its Valor Awards.

As Loudoun moves into a new century with heady possibilities, the Chamber seeks to strengthen its role as a stakeholder in the county's future. New office space—with critical and necessary technological enhancement—will assist its mission as the voice of business. Chamber participation in political forums with other regional Chambers will be increasingly vital, as is its membership in the Northern Virginia Coalition of Chambers of Commerce. With an active Technology Committee, it will strengthen services to Loudoun's burgeoning high-tech business community. And a strategic planning process will solicit the collective wisdom of Chamber members in crafting a future that meets the continuum of business needs in Loudoun County. It's an exciting time to be a Chamber member. ◼

Every other year, the Chamber honors Loudoun's fire, rescue, and law enforcement personnel with an event featuring its Valor Awards. Photo by David Galen.

The Loudoun County Chamber recognizes the efforts of the small business community with an annual awards program. In 1999, Patowmack Farms received the AgriBusiness of the Year Award. Photo by David Galen.

Loudoun

Loudoun County Government

Quality of life, achieved through strategic planning, is highly valued in Loudoun County. Well over 90 percent of citizens consistently rate Loudoun's quality of life as good or excellent. Board Chairman Scott York (left) discusses Loudoun's future with Vice Chairman Eleanore Towe and County Administrator Kirby Bowers.

Excellence in the classroom is a community expectation. Loudoun County spends more than 60 percent of its budget on public education. Citizens give education a satisfaction rating of 88 percent.

"We're all about building community. It's the common denominator that links all we do," says County Administrator Kirby Bowers, who supervises the day-to-day operations of county government. Guiding one of the fastest growing counties in the nation, the Loudoun County Government aggressively plans for the county's future as a premier technology center, a model of a thriving rural economy, and a community with a strong sense of place.

"The residents of Loudoun County are the envy of many communities," says Scott York, Chairman of the Loudoun County Board of Supervisors. "We live in a beautiful place. Our economy is booming. Unemployment is low. Innovative technology companies are locating here, making Loudoun County and Northern Virginia the global Internet capital."

Chairman York leads the nine-member Board of Supervisors that provides the overall policy and planning direction for the fastest growing large county in Virginia. With population increasing by about 1,000 new residents per month, citizens consider growth the number one issue. The current board, which began its four-year term in 2000, is determined to successfully manage growth.

The pace of growth, coupled with the community's beauty, technology businesses, and affordable housing, puts Loudoun in the vanguard of America's popular places to live. In 1990, the Loudoun County population was 86,000. By the year 2010, officials project a population of more than 300,000.

"A strong commercial and industrial tax base is important to help offset the cost of residential growth and to provide jobs for our citizens," says Board Chairman York. Current and projected increases in the commercial tax base help keep tax rates reasonable for residents while underwriting an aggressive program of community facilities for education, recreation, and public safety. This growing financial strength gives Loudoun consistently high bond ratings to build these community facilities.

Business and fiscal prosperity are priorities for the entire government. The county uses a team approach to economic development and involves all the key departments. Leading this effort, the Department of Economic Development focuses on creating a competitive edge in attracting, retaining, and growing business. Nationally recognized as one of the top 10 economic development organizations, the department provides "red-carpet" treatment to new and existing businesses wanting to grow in Loudoun.

County leaders are justifiably proud of both their record of stable and favorable tax rates to create an environment for business growth, and the personalized service the county provides in assisting business customers. Corporate executives say they can't believe they're dealing with government: "We had a very tight timetable to work against, and Loudoun County removed the barriers," says an America Online executive.

To create an economically competitive community, many new and existing business leaders seek to join top government and civic leaders on the 27-member Loudoun County Economic Development Commission, the principal economic development advisors to the Board of Supervisors. This energetic public-private commission hosts a monthly forum for important discussion of economic development strategies and action. These meetings, which are open to the public, are typically packed with interested business leaders and private citizens.

To "grow gracefully," good planning is one of Loudoun's highest priorities.

Blending Tradition With Innovation

Loudoun's Planning Director Julie Pastor says, "With a long history of planning for Loudoun's future development, we seek creative solutions to balance preservation of our natural, historic, and cultural resources with the county's continuing growth and development. In doing so, we tap strong civic leadership through our Planning Commission and the citizens who participate with us in planning for Loudoun's future."

The Planning Commission and the Board of Supervisors measure success not only in the overall quality of life they deliver but also in protecting and enhancing the assets that make Loudoun special: its wealth of natural beauty, the charming small towns, the high quality mixed-use communities, and Washington Dulles International Airport. Government leaders recognize the importance of the airport to Loudoun's economic future and have crafted nationally recognized strategies to support its development.

Loudoun County's success is not a fluke. Strong leadership, strategic planning, and good services are the county government's recipe for a great quality of life. County government, with headquarters in historic downtown Leesburg, is organized around five department clusters: public safety, community development, community services, finance, and internal operations.

A full spectrum of community services—from libraries to senior centers to mental health, social services, and public safety—meets a diverse population's needs. For example, the growing library system, ranked among the top systems in the country, provides handsome facilities for research and browsing, sophisticated technology to serve citizens in the library, and Internet capabilities that offer many library resources and databases directly to homes and businesses. Loudoun's citizens value the safety ensured by county services. They appreciate enhanced 911 emergency coverage, and the highly responsive Sheriff's Office and Fire and Rescue Services.

Loudoun's citizens expect the best in education. So do business leaders who consider starting, expanding, or locating their enterprises in Loudoun. Nationally normed achievement test scores have consistently ranked Loudoun's public schools' performance among the top 10 of Virginia's 130 school systems.

An elected school board is charged with delivering instruction and learning environments of the highest quality, while the county's Board of Supervisors provides most of the funding for the schools. State-of-the-art computer technology provides controlled access to the global resources of the Internet in all classrooms, laboratories, and libraries. Loudoun's schools are doing the right thing: more than 85 percent of the county's students continue their formal education after high school graduation.

The community and county government are committed to the preservation of Loudoun's rural character and way of life. Farmers credit the county's Land Use taxation program as one essential component in helping keep over 1,000 farms in Loudoun's 517 square miles. Agricultural land attracts visitors to equestrian events, the many wineries, and the annual spring and fall farm tours sponsored by the County. County leaders expect to double the value of the rural economy in the next decade. County staff and knowledgeable consultants will help "techs and execs" bring compatible technology businesses to rural Loudoun, new businesses open in the small towns, and farmers take advantage of the latest techniques to keep agriculture—from horse, cattle, and llama farms to vegetable farms—profitable and flourishing.

In this, the first decade of the twenty-first century, county leaders envision a community that benefits from a strong business base, well-planned suburban communities, and a remarkable rural quality of life—a county that, in a way, represents the American dream. County Administrator Kirby Bowers challenges the County government to help build a great community: "When the rankings are made of the top 20 quality of life communities, we want Loudoun to be on those lists." ◢

Volunteers and career professionals provide fire and rescue services. Citizens give them a 99-percent satisfaction rating.

Loudoun's citizens enjoy getting together at one of the many community centers that are part of the Department of Parks, Recreation, and Community Services. Citizens give it a satisfaction rating of more than 90 percent. Photos by David Galen.

113

Loudoun

Blending Tradition With Innovation

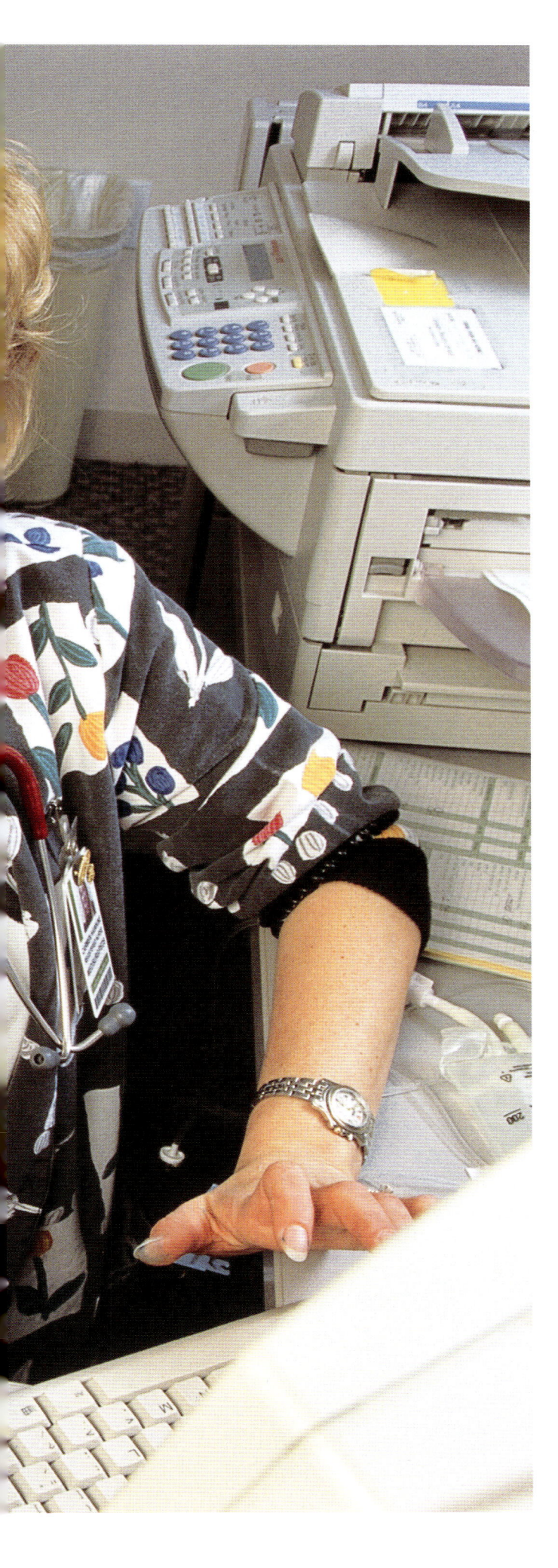

Chapter Thirteen

Health and Education

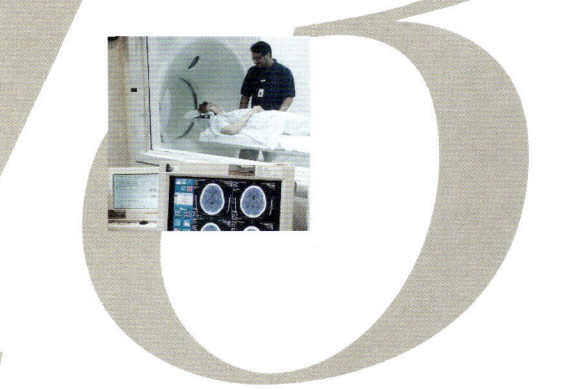

13

Loudoun Healthcare, Inc., 116-117
Reston Hospital Center, 118-119
Foxcroft School, 120-121

Outstanding health care and a fine educational system add to Loudoun County's exceptional quality of life. Photo by David Galen.

115

Loudoun Healthcare, Inc.

With the opening of a six-room hospital in 1912, Loudoun County's citizens made a commitment to community-based health care. This commitment has grown as steadily as the county itself. Independent, not-for-profit Loudoun Healthcare, Inc. is now recognized as one of the Commonwealth's leading community care networks.

Loudoun Hospital Center's new medical center opened in October 1997 at Lansdowne.

Medical staff member emeritus William P. Frazer, M.D. and former Chiefs of Staff John Archer, M.D. and Anthony Crowley, M.D. unveil the cornerstone at the new Loudoun Hospital Center during ceremonies on May 19, 1996. Photo by David Galen.

In the century's first decade, Loudoun resident P. Howell Lightfoot canvassed the countryside on horseback to arouse interest in a county hospital. Local physicians William C. Orr and John A. Gibson met in Horace Littlejohn's Leesburg pharmacy to lay plans, and soon a rented house became Leesburg Hospital. True to Loudoun's personality, the first patient was a jockey thrown from his horse.

The organizers knew they'd need help with housekeeping and fund-raising if the hospital was to succeed, so they turned to Loudoun's ladies. "Unless you women go along," Dr. Gibson told Miss Alice Davis and Mrs. William Corcoran Eustis, "we'll not attempt it."

He need not have worried; the promptly formed Ladies Board invited the public to donate money and supplies, and the citizens happily obliged. Responsibility for the housekeeping and kitchen remained with the Ladies Board for many years, as they worked with the Leesburg Garden Club to grow and can vegetables for hospital patients and staff.

The Ladies Board also supported early expansion of hospital programs, including the first rural visiting nurse service in Virginia. Enthusiastic fund-raising enabled the purchase of land and the construction of a larger hospital in 1918.

During Loudoun County's rapid growth in the post-World War II years, the hospital underwent repeated expansion, thanks largely to the generosity of area residents. In the 1960s, the hospital's future was assured when it received Medicare certification and an extraordinarily bountiful bequest.

Additional hospital expansions in the '70s and '80s accompanied new ancillary services, such as a nursing home, the "Lifeline" connection between the emergency department and elderly and disabled county residents, and community outreach programs. In 1985 Loudoun Healthcare, Inc. (LHI) was formed as the parent corporation of the hospital—now Loudoun Hospital Center—and its growing number of affiliates.

Today, these affiliates ensure quality care across the largest county in Virginia. With a stunning new 80-bed facility at Lansdowne, Loudoun Healthcare still maintains a presence in downtown Leesburg with its Behavioral Health Unit, Long-Term Care Center, and Rehabilitation Services. Loudoun Healthcare serves old-timers and newcomers, with its medical staff membership of over 365 physicians, and an impressive array of health education and management classes. The comprehensive Expectant Family Series is particularly popular.

Loudoun Healthcare's Mobile Health Services travels throughout the county to provide medical care, screenings, immunizations, and health and safety education. The Mobile Health Van is a frequent visitor in various parts of the county, targeting those who are medically underserved, as well as the general public and corporate clients.

Blending Tradition With Innovation

Loudoun Healthcare's Emergency Services coordinates critical care delivery in the Emergency Department with highly trained EMS volunteers across the county. This partnership of care provided by EMS personnel and hospital staff guarantees seamless delivery in critical moments for Loudoun's residents.

Accessible care is available in western Loudoun County at the Purcellville Physical Medicine and Rehabilitation and in the Loudoun Valley Medical Center, which also includes the affiliated diagnostic imaging at the Women's Center and physician offices.

In eastern Loudoun County, site of much of the region's unprecedented growth, the highly regarded Loudoun Cancer Care Center offers a full range of diagnostic and treatment programs within a holistic framework of education and support. LHI's Countryside Ambulatory Surgery Center, NOVA Urgent Care in Sterling, and the affiliated Sterling/Dulles Imaging and MRI Center also serve this dynamic community.

Loudoun Healthcare's commitment to quality is demonstrable. Its facilities attract top-notch clinicians; more than 92 percent of the active medical staff are Board Certified in their specialties. Ongoing patient satisfaction evaluations consistently place Loudoun Hospital Center above comparable hospitals nationwide. Its numerous awards include the American Lung Association's Partner of the Year and recognition by the American Heart Association and the American Diabetes Association. The county Chamber of Commerce named LHI the Corporate Citizen of the Year.

Maintaining close community ties is a priority. Loudoun Healthcare's leaders are involved in the public schools, the Chamber of Commerce, and numerous local boards and foundations. Its award-winning cooperative relationship with the Monroe Technology Center trains Licensed Practical Nurses, a win-win arrangement for both the hospital and those who seek careers in nursing.

LHI also gives back to the community through support of health-related organizations and youth and senior citizen programs.

The support of the Ladies Board continues today through the thrift shop, rummage sale, nursing scholarships, and the Hospital Gift Shop. Profits from Ladies Board activities enable purchases of cutting-edge medical equipment. Their work supports Loudoun Healthcare's commitment to serve all who need its care, regardless of ability to pay. LHI's charity care exceeds $1.2 million annually.

Loudoun Healthcare's philanthropic division, Loudoun Healthcare Foundation, is responsible for meeting the fund-raising goals set by the board of directors of Loudoun Healthcare, Inc. and serves as the primary advocate for Loudoun Healthcare in the community. The foundation is in the process of becoming a separately incorporated subsidiary of Loudoun Healthcare. Donors may direct their contributions to specific areas of interest or make unrestricted donations. They are assured their gifts are managed by the board and staff of the foundation focused to meet the needs of donors in support of Loudoun Healthcare. The staff can provide easy to understand information to anyone interested in supporting the community hospital.

Loudoun Healthcare, Inc. employs 1,200 people in full- and part-time positions, consistently placing it among the top five employers in the county. More than 400 adult volunteers and 100 junior volunteers contributed over 38,000 hours of service in 1998 alone. Volunteers serve as valuable resources in over 50 areas of the organization, and are ever ready to assist with any project—small or large.

Loudoun Healthcare is positioning to meet the demands of the county's population boom. Its growth has been reflective of the county's changes, and services have been designed and located in response to meeting community needs. The recent relocation of the hospital to the demographic center of the county—with an eye to future expansion—demonstrates this strategic vision.

LHI's volunteer board of directors has reaffirmed its desire for the system to remain a community-based, not-for-profit organization. Such determination makes Loudoun Healthcare, Inc. a hallmark of Loudoun County's spirit.

Brian Krikalo, junior volunteer, visits with hospital greeting desk volunteers Margaret James and Dorothy Rowe. Photo by David Galen.

Enjoying a workout in Loudoun Hospital Center's Cardiopulmonary Health Center are George Wenrich and Ruth Wise. Photo by David Galen.

Loudoun

Reston Hospital Center

Reston Hospital Center, a full-service medical/surgical hospital, opened in November 1986, and is located within Reston's vibrant Town Center complex. More than 275 physicians, both primary care and specialists, have offices on the hospital campus.

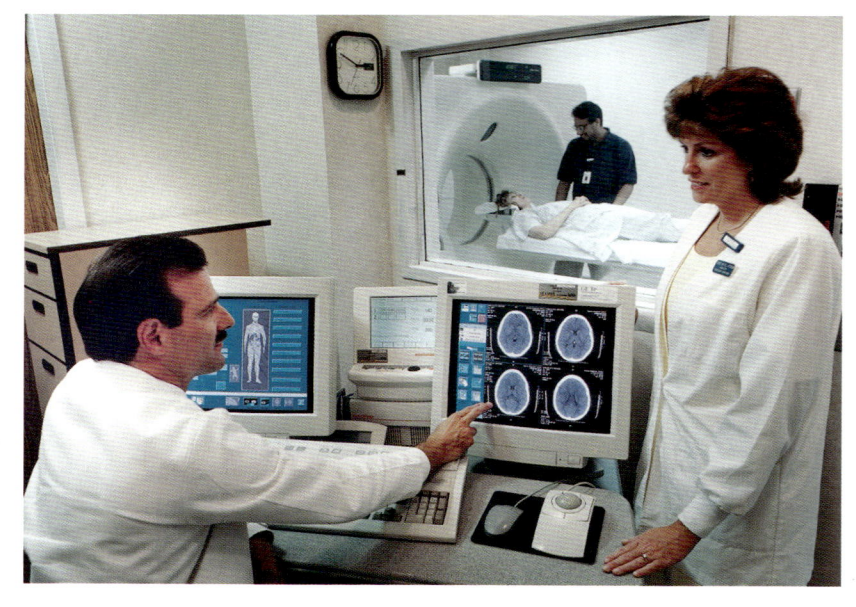

The latest generation of Computed Tomography (CT) equipment reformats views for better evaluation by radiologists at Reston Hospital Center.

Established in 1986, Reston Hospital Center is a sophisticated, full-service community hospital that provides hometown care. The hospital campus is in Reston's exciting Town Center, close to shops and businesses—Reston is western Fairfax County's thriving planned community adjacent to Loudoun County. The 127-bed facility serves both counties and gives Loudoun citizens a choice of hospital care.

A privately owned, tax-paying hospital, Reston Hospital Center is part of the Columbia/HCA Healthcare System based in Nashville, Tennessee. The hospital takes pride in being a well-managed community institution that values the stewardship of its resources. It recognizes that the well-educated populace has high expectations and expects the best in medical care.

Reston Hospital Center serves the community with 24-hour emergency care and high volume surgical services. It offers a comprehensive range of medical/surgical services that include critical and progressive care units. The hospital is known for its very busy maternal/child services and outpatient surgery; more than 80 percent of surgical cases are now "same day" procedures. The urology department offers a state-of-the-art lithotripter for dissolving kidney stones, thereby reducing the need for surgery and lengthy recovery time. A strong program in orthopedics and rehabilitation medicine includes a strong physical therapy department with a medically supervised fitness program.

With the recent addition of a radiation therapy department that includes a skilled staff and the most advanced technology, the hospital has become a true cancer treatment center. It provides surgery, chemotherapy, and radiation therapy in one location so that area residents can have the full scope of sophisticated cancer care in their own neighborhood. At a time when people feel most vulnerable, the hospital's moderate size assures a non-threatening environment and patient-friendly care.

More than 750 primary care and specialty physicians have privileges at Reston Hospital Center, and many of them maintain practices in both Loudoun and Fairfax Counties. Medical office buildings on the hospital campus include convenient offices for 275 physicians. "We have a strong, dedicated medical staff," says a hospital spokesperson. "They are excited about their work and in the prime of their practice."

The hospital employs 1,000 people; it is an accessible employer for its 225 full- and part-time employees from Loudoun County. A strong and growing cadre of 200 volunteers contribute their time and talent to every aspect of the hospital program, including neighborhood outreach programs.

Blending Tradition With Innovation

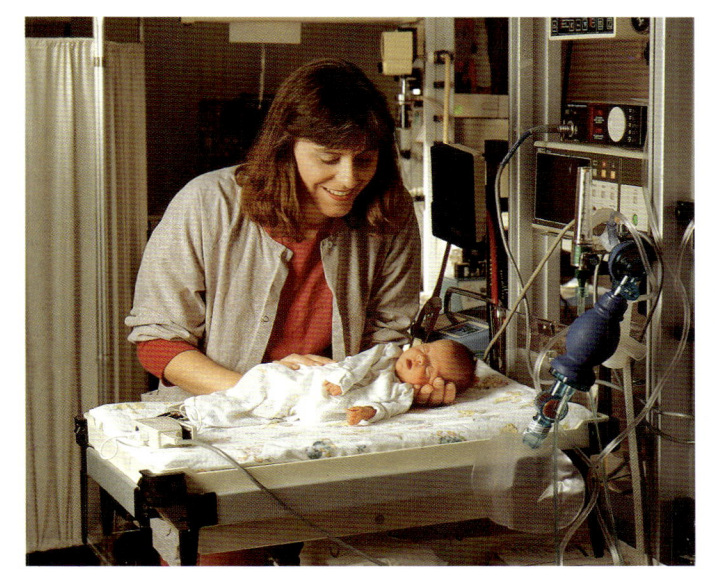

Reston Hospital's menu of health and wellness programs include "Healthy Communities," which provides free or low-cost screenings for stroke, prostate, and breast cancer, and other potentially threatening diseases. Screening detects illness in early, treatable stages, and the hospital makes the screenings available to area businesses as an employee benefit.

Reston Hospital Center holds a wide variety of support groups for cardiac, diabetic, and cancer patients and their families. Hospital staff members facilitate an Ethics Day at area high schools to expose students to ethical decision making in health-related issues. A full schedule of health and wellness classes for the community includes CPR and first aid, weight loss and fitness, childbirth and sibling preparation, osteoporosis, diabetes, mental health, smoking cessation, and women's health. And a vibrant membership program for seniors provides health and fitness support. It reaches more than 850 members who enjoy programs, screenings, and trips.

After years of intensive focus on quality improvement by the entire staff, Reston Hospital Center's patients give it high marks for the quality of its nursing professionals, the accessibility of ancillary services such as physical therapy and radiology, and even the hospital food. It is accredited by the Joint Commission on Accreditation of Healthcare Organizations.

Reston Hospital Center has embarked on an ambitious $35.2-million expansion project. The innovative plans include a three-story addition and the reallocation of existing space to provide a more efficient infrastructure to streamline all patient services. Since the number of births at the hospital is expected to reach 3,000 per year in the near future—many Loudoun County babies are born at Reston Hospital—the plans include an entirely new maternity center. "Giving birth is a special experience and with this addition, we will be able to provide families with the environment that they would like," says one official.

The improvements reflect the changing medical needs in the community with a conversion of all 127 beds to private rooms, expanded surgery and critical care capabilities, and additional classrooms. A new parking building will increase the number of available parking spaces to nearly 1,100. The expansion is scheduled for completion by 2003.

Reston Hospital Center has received awards for service and business excellence from the Greater Reston Chamber of Commerce and Reston Interfaith. Its leadership participates in the Chambers of Commerce within its service area and encourages all employees to be actively engaged in the community. Staff members are involved in fund-raising activities such as the Relay for Life, American Cancer Society, and the Heart Association.

Reston Hospital Center is well positioned to weather the changes in health care regulations and reimbursement and to meet growing community needs in the new century. "When it comes right down to it, we are neighbors taking care of neighbors," says Claudia Smith, the hospital's director of public relations. "We believe you can get extraordinary, personalized care here on a manageable scale." ◼

Caring for the area's youngest and smallest residents is a big job for the nurses in Reston Hospital Center's Maternity Center. More than 2,000 babies are born there each year.

Reston Hospital Center is undergoing a major renovation project to better serve patients in the western Fairfax and eastern Loudoun area. The construction project will allow all patients to have a private room. The entire Maternal/Child Health unit will be streamlined, and a parking structure will be added for better patient and visitor access to services.

Loudoun

Foxcroft School

Foxcroft, a girls' boarding school for grades 9 through 12, is among the new breed of educational institutions that dispel old stereotypes and exemplify the "girls' school advantage." Quality is evident not only in its gracious hunt-country campus near Middleburg, but also in the achievements of its students.

Quality is evident not only in Foxcroft School's gracious hunt-country campus near Middleburg, but also in the achievements of its students.

Foxcroft School was founded in 1914 by Charlotte Haxall Noland, a Loudoun County woman well ahead of her time. She envisioned a school that would set distinctive standards for intellectual and moral honesty, hard work, sense of self, sense of purpose, and joy of life. "Miss Charlotte" laid the cornerstone for the Leesburg Hospital, was the first female Master of the Middleburg Hunt, and was a founding director of the Middleburg Bank. She challenged others to examine ways to improve themselves and the world around them by thinking in nontraditional ways.

Foxcroft is the embodiment of Miss Charlotte's vision; academic excellence, leadership, responsibility, and integrity are its stated values. On its 500-acre campus 50 miles west of Washington, D.C., Foxcroft offers a rigorous college preparatory program for 165 girls who reflect a diversity that exceeds many of northern Virginia's public schools. Its international program attracts foreign students, as well. Eighty-five percent of Foxcroft's students are boarders. Endowed scholarships ensure a well-rounded student body with over half a million dollars in annual need-based financial assistance and with several merit-based scholarships.

Foxcroft offers a rigorous college preparatory program for 165 girls who reflect a diversity that exceeds many of northern Virginia's public schools. Photo by Bill Denison.

Research demonstrates that girls learn more effectively connecting with, relating to, and affiliating with the material and with other learners, and Foxcroft students do learn in collaboration with other students and their teachers. The maximum class size is 15, and the 6-to-1 student-to-faculty ratio encourages participation and lively debate. Nearly half of Foxcroft's 31 full-time educators hold advanced degrees in their fields, and more than 90 percent of the teachers live on campus. These same teachers serve as club sponsors, coaches, faithful fans, enthusiastic audiences, and, most important, mentors and role models.

Head of School Mary Louise Leipheimer explains: "Our faculty teaches students that they are valued, not just because they do well in class but because of who they are. The girl who may be having trouble in one class will see that teacher cheering for her at a lacrosse game, and she knows that she has someone who wants her to succeed."

Students meet the standards of a directed liberal arts curriculum with a remarkably broad range of electives for a school of its size. Foxcroft's Senior Thesis encourages independent interdisciplinary research in much the same way as a postgraduate exercise, and students orally present and defend their original work. Off-campus activities, such as trips to Princeton University Plasma/Fusion Laboratory and Washington's Walter Reed Medical Museum of Science, enrich science students. "The Write Place" develops young writers, using advanced computer and networking skills to teach the interdisciplinary nature of information. And the fine arts are well-served with a variety of solo, ensemble, and performance opportunities and with the studio arts.

Interim Term is an example of Foxcroft's emphasis on competencies that last a lifetime. Two weeks each year, issue-oriented programs with a global focus offer experiential learning that promotes critical thinking and decision-making. Cocurricular programs like the annual Poetry Festival and the Goodyear Fellowship Program bring such world-class fellows and poets as Maya Angelou, Jean-Michel Cousteau, Barbara Walters, Richard Leakey, and Archibald MacLeish to campus.

Since Middleburg and horsemanship are nearly synonymous, Foxcroft has a strong riding program. Foxcroft's founder believed that riding teaches responsibility and develops the ability to make decisions. Students use a 60-stall stable, indoor and outdoor arenas, and paddocks to board their own horses or enjoy one of Foxcroft's mounts. Riding can meet the physical education requirement, and may become a pleasurable pastime or a highly skilled, competitive activity—the team consistently earns the highest recognition in regional trials and shows. The student Riding Club assists the riding staff in planning and managing equestrian events and in supervising beginning riders. But one does not have to be a rider. There are varsity and junior varsity teams in field hockey, volleyball, cross-country, basketball, soccer, lacrosse, softball, and tennis.

No one can argue that the Foxcroft years are not challenging and enjoyable. But the proof is in the results, and they are impressive. In a recent graduating class, more than 90 percent of the students were accepted to their top choice colleges, and more than 40 percent of these received merit scholarships totaling more than $880,000.

Cumulative SAT scores are consistently more than 100 points above the national norm for girls. The majority of seniors are enrolled in advanced placement courses, and almost 100 percent graduate with four years or more of math and science. It is no wonder that applications to Foxcroft are growing at an extraordinary rate.

Foxcroft's Loudoun County location supports its mission. Among hills that seem to roll on forever and with a small-town environment, girls feel safe enough to discover their own power. The immediacy of nature enhances programs in environmental studies; with their eye on locally treasured Goose Creek, the girls monitor the school's own sewage treatment plant. Proximity to the nation's capital presents endless possibilities for historical and cultural day trips.

Service is part of the Foxcroft ethic, and the girls give back to their community. More than 40 students are involved in Leesburg's Special Friends program, with many others helping out at the local humane society and women's shelter, working with Habitat for Humanity, or tutoring at nearby schools. Foxcroft's library, one of the largest in the county at 50,000 volumes, is open to the entire community, as is the Duncan H. Read Observatory, a gift from a generous Foxcroft neighbor.

The region's growing population and economy are encouraging renewed strategic thinking at Foxcroft. "We want to be good neighbors; it's part of what we teach," says Leipheimer. The school is examining expansion of its five-day program to welcome increasing numbers of Loudoun County's new education-oriented families.

Foxcroft models an educational environment founded on women's ways of learning, doing, and interacting. It is a place where risk-taking is encouraged, community is valued, and success is always possible. ◼

Foxcroft's library is one of the largest in the county and boasts 50,000 volumes. Photo by Bill Denison.

Foxcroft offers varsity and junior varsity teams in field hockey, volleyball, cross-country, basketball, soccer, lacrosse, softball, tennis, and riding. Photo by Bill Denison.

Loudoun

Blending Tradition With Innovation

Chapter Fourteen

The Marketplace

Raspberry Falls Golf and Hunt Club, 124-125
The Holiday Inn at Historic Carradoc Hall, 126-127
Lansdowne Resort, 128-129

The area's retail establishments and service industries vitalize Loudoun County's economic life. Photo by David Galen.

Loudoun

Raspberry Falls Golf and Hunt Club

Raspberry Falls Golf and Hunt Club has the character of a challenging Scottish-style course. Photo by Mark Brown.

Raspberry is a fine example of the "country club for a day" concept, and it works well for Loudoun County. Photo by Mark Brown.

Although Loudoun County increasingly exhibits an accelerated lifestyle, old and new residents still cherish its genteel traditions. At an acclaimed daily-fee golf club nestled against the foothills of the Blue Ridge, you will find every accommodation for today's busy leisure golfers with a large helping of Southern service and hospitality—what you might expect from the finest membership club. Add the character of a challenging Scottish-style course, and you have Raspberry Falls Golf and Hunt Club.

Adjacent to the historic Raspberry Plains plantation and with other fine old properties visible from the course, the club recalls the grace of bygone days. From the moment you turn through the imposing gateway just a few miles north of Leesburg, it is clear that no expense has been spared to provide golfers with a memorable experience. A generous two-tiered practice facility appears on the left side of the drive before the plantation clubhouse comes into view. Uniformed attendants immediately appear to welcome you, take care of your clubs, and answer any questions. After your game, you will enjoy swapping tales with fellow golfers over a cool drink on the back porch, or perhaps over a fine meal in the mahogany-paneled club room. A well-appointed pro shop is close at hand.

The club's coexistence with the local fox hunt is a unique addition to the ambiance. There may be no other top-flight golf facility in the nation where baying hounds can interrupt play on the fairway, red-coated fox hunters in hot pursuit. When locating the course near the Loudoun West Hunt Club with a long tradition of riding the land, Raspberry Falls' developers chose to turn a potential problem into an asset. "After all," says General Manager Bob Swiger, "we came to their backyard." This is Virginia.

Raspberry Falls is a good neighbor to area businesses and community groups as well. An increasingly popular venue for corporate golf outings and Christmas parties, it also accommodates events with a hometown flavor, like the AAAA high school state championships, the Loudoun County Chamber of Commerce tournament, and numerous charitable functions.

Raspberry is a fine example of the "country club for a day" concept, and it works well for Loudoun County. As Swiger explains it, the membership club era has somewhat faded, when the comfortably fixed executive spent time on his country club's links while his wife watched the kids at poolside. "Today, we've got a lot of men, women, and their children who like to golf, but their free time is far more limited and they travel frequently—a club membership doesn't make sense," says Swiger. "That doesn't mean they don't want that kind of service and environment when they do play. And they'll find it every time they come to Raspberry Falls."

"That kind of service" translates to the arrival on the course of iced-down towels during a hot afternoon round, or the welcome appearance of attendants with steaming clam chowder at the seventh hole when the Virginia mountain chill sets in. The customer-oriented Raspberry staff clean players' clubs at the end of the round, and members-for-a-day depart with shoes shined and cars freshly washed, if requested. By keeping traffic to an average of 40,000 rounds each year, Raspberry's management knows it can provide service consistency and take good care of its bentgrass, the gold standard in golf turf.

Success in providing the look and feel of a country club has certainly not diluted Raspberry Falls' emphasis on good golf. Opening to critical acclaim in 1996, the 7,191-yard, par-72 course was developed by Stradinger & Swiger, a firm with considerable Myrtle Beach golf success to its credit. Raspberry Falls is a signature course, the first in Virginia to be designed by Gary Player (also a horseman), who knew how to capitalize on the area's stunning terrain. Raspberry's staff does not skimp on keeping the course in top shape. With five sets of tee markers, wide fairways, long par-fours and gentle greens, these links take every advantage of elevation changes. Raspberry's teaching pro and assistants are there to make you comfortable with your game, whether you are a once-a-year duffer or a frequent, earnest player.

One of a very few regional courses with bentgrass from tee to green, its open feel and stacked-sod bunkers are typical of the Scottish golfing tradition. The nearly vertical bunkers add character, but players can attest to their challenge; some shots need to be played out sideways or backwards. The third tee offers a great course overview from its 100-foot rise. Civil War-era stone walls were reconstructed on several holes, and the par-five ninth hole, the Citadel, adds a creek and a formidable bunker. The eleventh hole is 590 yards of physical golf, with Lee's Bunker guarding the front of the green and Grant's Tomb on the right. The back nine appeals to the low handicappers, while the front feels more welcoming to the occasional golfer. If the mark of a good golf course is how many holes you'll remember, then Raspberry Falls, with its bunkers, vertical drops, mountain views, stone outcroppings, waterfalls, and babbling brook is one great course.

Small wonder that Raspberry Falls has garnered quick acceptance and approval. With a four-star rating from *Golf Digest*, it has also been named among the top 10 mid-Atlantic courses and the national top 50 for service, including private clubs. It has been written up in virtually every golfing publication. As Northern Virginia accommodates its growing populace with first-class recreational facilities and explores its potential as a golf destination, Loudoun County has a winner in Raspberry Falls. ◢

Raspberry Falls is a signature course, the first in Virginia to be designed by Gary Player, who knew how to capitalize on the area's stunning terrain. Photo by Mark Brown.

With a four-star rating from **Golf Digest**, *Raspberry Falls has been named among the top 10 mid-Atlantic courses and the national top 50 for service, including private clubs. Photo by Mark Brown.*

The Holiday Inn at Historic Carradoc Hall

Like no Holiday Inn anywhere, Leesburg's Holiday Inn at Historic Carradoc Hall offers an authentic mansion more than 200 year old and modern guest facilities—a mirror of Loudoun County's unique marriage of history and progress.

Originally an estate owned by the Newton and Harper families, Carradoc Hall's history dates back more than 200 years, when Captain Willoughby Newton purchased part of Henry "Lighthorse" Lee's Belmont Plantation. Carradoc was the original Welsh name of the Newton family. Robert Newton Harper, Leesburg businessman and pharmacist, was locally famous at the turn of the century for Harper's Headache Medicine.

When 122 guest rooms and a tavern were added after a 1984 purchase, the property became an inn. In June 1997, Carradoc Hall was bought by Crown American Hotels in Johnstown, Pennsylvania, one of the mid-Atlantic's top hotel management and development corporations. Crown American operates hotels through franchise agreements, and in early 1998, Carradoc Hall became a Holiday Inn.

To provide patrons with the best in accommodations, Crown American invested $1.7 million dollars in renovation, comfort features, and landscaping on eight scenic acres. Every effort was made to preserve Carradoc Hall's historic ambiance.

The lobby area welcomes visitors with a cozy fireplace. Visitors have their choice of accommodations—modern guest rooms or Mansion Suites. All accommodations include convenience amenities and a voice messaging system. The four historically restored Mansion Suites, on the second floor of the original structure, offer a bed-and-breakfast experience. Each has a parlor and period furnishings. The suites are popular with honeymooners and business travelers seeking genteel Virginia hospitality. Every inn visitor is welcome to use the fitness room, seasonal outdoor pool, and the gazebo, walks, and porches that overlook the land.

Two distinct dining experiences, both owned and operated by Crown American Hotels, are popular with visitors and area residents alike. The Lighthorse Tavern serves relaxing cocktails and light fare in an inviting pub setting. The Mansion House Restaurant is in the original Carradoc Hall, and takes full advantage of its history. Using antiques and careful reproductions, the small dining rooms provide discerning diners with an experience one might only expect in the quaintest antebellum inn. Far from standard motel fare, the Mansion House Restaurant serves continental and contemporary American cuisine, often featuring lamb, veal, and seafood. The restaurant is a popular contributor to the Taste of Loudoun each year.

The inn is a favorite for business travelers who depend on its peace and quiet. Off-duty pilots at Dulles Airport pass by several hotels to take advantage of the Holiday Inn's restful atmosphere; warm weather often finds airline personnel with a good book and a cool drink on the verandah. Rooms feature data ports and outlets in desk lamp bases, eliminating the need in many other facilities to move furniture and unplug phones. Hourly complimentary shuttle service makes connecting with Dulles flights easy.

The Holiday Inn at Historic Carradoc Hall is perfect for small corporate meetings, offering a real escape from the usual business environment. With conference and banquet facilities that accommodate 300 and smaller rooms for informal meetings and breakout sessions, meeting planners find the inn conducive to productivity. The yard, terraces, and gazebo are often used for discussions, as well. The experienced staff assists in conference planning and secures the necessary support services.

History buffs find that the inn's location is handy for exploring the region's battlefields and historic sites. The inn recently

Blending Tradition With Innovation

hosted a Civil War study group from the Smithsonian Institution. Shoppers appreciate the proximity to quaint shops and antiquing in historic Leesburg, the Leesburg Corner Premium Outlets, and the new Dulles Town Center—all within a 15-minute drive. Or the staff can arrange a relaxing round of golf at nearby Raspberry Falls Golf and Hunt Club or the Lansdowne Resort.

The Holiday Inn at Carradoc Hall is nearly a second home to the Loudoun County Chamber of Commerce, with three or four committee meetings held there each week. Other regular business customers include the Dulles Area Association of Realtors.

The inn's management believes that what makes the Holiday Inn at Historic Carradoc Hall special is its place in the community's life. "We hear so often that families have had weddings and reunions here over the years," says a spokesman. "It is wonderful to be part of the continuum of family history."

Community involvement is good business for the inn. It has been the site of events to help the United Way, March of Dimes, and the Boy Scouts. Local fire and rescue squads are honored there at annual banquets. The Salvation Army holds a dinner at the inn to honor volunteers each year, and a fund-raiser for the Muscular Dystrophy Association featured baked goods by the staff. The management team also pitches in for the annual Community Holiday Coalition food drive.

Crown American's investment in melding modern amenities with Loudoun County's history has been rewarded. Honored with Bass Hotels & Resorts' Newcomer of the Year Award in 1998, the inn followed this success with the 1999 Quality Excellence Award, given only to hotels achieving distinction in all aspects of their operations. The Holiday Inn at Historic Carradoc Hall offers Loudoun County quality that makes it a gracious home away from home.

To provide patrons with the best in accommodations, Crown American invested $1.7 million dollars in renovation, comfort features, and landscaping on eight scenic acres. Every effort was made to preserve Carradoc Hall's historic ambiance.

Loudoun

Lansdowne Resort

Lansdowne Resort's convenient location, Robert Trent Jones Jr. championship golf course, extraordinary appointments, and spectacular setting make it a unique destination for both conference and leisure activities.

Lansdowne Resort is managed by Benchmark Hospitality, a Texas-based company that boasts some of the country's premier resorts and conference facilities.

Loudoun County's Lansdowne Resort is the Washington, D.C., area's only full-service Four Diamond resort. Its convenient location, Robert Trent Jones Jr. championship golf course, extraordinary appointments, and spectacular setting make Lansdowne a unique destination for both conference and leisure activities.

Resting against Virginia's hunt country near historic Leesburg, Virginia, Lansdowne's Potomac River panorama and mountain views invite relaxation. Visitors who want to explore the area have the options of Civil War battlefields, Loudoun County vineyards, plantations, and equestrian centers, Leesburg's antique shops, and Wolf Trap Farm Park—the national park for the performing arts. Washington, D.C., is only 25 miles away. Eight miles from Washington Dulles International Airport, the resort is easily accessible to travelers.

Lansdowne's corporate customers know they can expect the very best in accommodations and conference facilities. The 305 deluxe rooms and suites—all with their own handsome view—boast 2-line data-port phones and spacious work areas, making it a pleasure to do business. The 45,000-square-foot Executive Conference Center offers 25 meeting rooms for every need, including the Boardroom, break-out rooms, a 9,525-square-foot ballroom, and a 126-seat amphitheater. All conference space is wired for teleconferencing and has state-of-the-art audiovisual capabilities; the amphitheater is outfitted with Internet-ready analog ports. Convenient coffee break kiosks supply continuous refreshments.

Corporate meeting planners know they can delegate the details to Lansdowne, where conference planning managers leave nothing to chance, and a conference concierge attends to last-minute requests. In addition to the expected business services, Lansdowne's audiovisual studio can edit and duplicate videos and produce multimedia presentations. Custom meeting packages are available. From board meetings to team building to management retreats, Lansdowne is the key ingredient to success.

This resort is not all business. As a leisure destination, Lansdowne pampers guests in every way. The full-service health club features Heartline exercise equipment, a steam room, and sauna. The Spa at Lansdowne offers a full menu of massages and salon services. Tennis, racquetball, and volleyball courts are in ample supply, and swimming is easy year-round, with both indoor and outdoor pools. Nature trails display the beauty of the land and the river for quiet strolls, brisk runs, or mountain biking. The Resort Rascals™ program can keep youngsters happily entertained weekdays, weekends, and evenings, leaving parents to take full advantage of Lansdowne's many features.

Golfers consider the resort's 18 holes some of the finest in the region. Designed by Robert Trent Jones Jr., the more than 7,000-yard, par-72 course incorporates natural stone outcroppings and the Potomac Valley woodlands. The elevation change at the finishing hole provides a dramatic conclusion for any golfer. Lansdowne's teaching pros are available for tips, and the well-stocked pro shop, driving range, and chipping and putting greens complete the experience.

Blending Tradition With Innovation

Lansdowne's restaurants, the Riverside Hearth and the Lansdowne Grille, serve up regional favorites and some of Loudoun County's best steaks. The chefs even offer cooking classes. The seasonal Fairways Deli, convenient to both swimmers and golfers, offers light fare, drinks, and snacks that can be enjoyed on the covered deck with a fine cigar. Just off the living room, Stonewalls Tavern is an inviting place for drinks, billiards, and darts, or a friendly visit near the massive fieldstone fireplace or the large-screen television.

Area residents enjoy Lansdowne's popular packages for getting away from busy schedules. Whether it's the golf or spa getaway, or the romance package with flowers, champagne, and breakfast in bed, northern Virginians always receive a warm welcome. "It's their resort," says a spokesperson. "People don't need to spend half their getaway traveling—it's right in their own backyard." Down home barbecues mark the summer holidays, and Halloween at Lansdowne means hayrides and games. Winter brings the gingerbread house contest that helps local schools gather canned goods for the area's interfaith relief effort. The resort staff can make Lansdowne a memorable celebration destination for any special event, from Mother's Day brunches to birthdays and weddings. Onsite catering can easily create banquets for 700 or intimate theme parties.

Lansdowne continues to offer the Executive Club, a preferred discount dining program. When members dine at Lansdowne, they receive a complimentary meal in any resort restaurant or a 25 percent discount. Additional benefits include a free weekday round of golf, health club visits, numerous discounts on Lansdowne activities, and a complimentary second night in a deluxe room.

A popular site for corporate golf outings and employee events, Lansdowne also serves as the venue for occasions that give back to the community. The Lansdowne Ballroom hosts many Loudoun County charitable events, like the benefits for the local Habitat for Humanity and the YMCA. Washington football legend Bobby Mitchell chooses Lansdowne for his successful annual Hall of Fame Golf Tournament to raise money for leukemia research.

A $4.5-million renovation, completed in spring 1999, brought new warmth and a comfortable elegance to the entire resort, as well as technology upgrades to the conference center. Lansdowne anticipates further expansion to meet the growing needs of a growing community—another golf course and expansion of the spa and ballroom are envisioned.

Lansdowne Resort is managed by Benchmark Hospitality, a Texas-based company that boasts some of the country's premier resorts and conference facilities. Benchmark's philosophy of living, learning, and leisure is evident in the high standards of every Lansdowne experience. In addition to the American Automobile Association's Four Diamond Award, the meeting industry has conferred numerous high honors: *Meetings and Conventions Magazine* gave Lansdowne its Gold Key Award, and the resort received Corporate and Incentive Travel's Paragon Award.

Golfers consider the resort's 18 holes some of the finest in the region. Designed by Robert Trent Jones Jr., the more than 7,000-yard, par-72 course incorporates natural stone outcroppings and the Potomac Valley woodlands.

Lansdowne's 305 deluxe rooms and suites—all with their own handsome view—boast 2-line dataport phones and spacious work areas, making it a pleasure to do business.

Bibliography

1998 Annual Growth Summary: Loudoun County, Virginia. Leesburg, Virginia: Department of Economic Development, 1999. Statistical information on all aspects of growth within Loudoun County in 1998.

Loudoun Handbook. Leesburg, Virginia: Handbooks, Inc., 1998. Handbook describing county history, services, communities, and annual events.

The 200,000 Acre Solution: Supporting and Enhancing a Rural Economy for Loudoun's 21st Century. Leesburg, Virginia: Loudoun County Department of Economic Development, 1998. A rural economic development plan for Loudoun County by the Rural Task Force.

Directories
Loudoun County Chamber of Commerce 1999 Business Directory/Resource Guide. Chesapeake, Virginia: Landmark Publishing, 1999. Business directory and resource guide for the county and chamber of commerce.

Sources
Bendure, Vicki. President. Communication Concepts, 201 E. Washington St., Middleburg, Virginia.

Collins, Randy. President. Loudoun County Chamber of Commerce, 5 Loudoun Street SW, Suite A, Leesburg, Virginia.

Converse, Molly. Public Information Officer. Loudoun Public School System, 102 North Street NW, Leesburg, Virginia.

Fragen, G. Frederick VMD. Marion Dupont Scott Equine Medical Center, Morven Park, Leesburg, Virginia.

Gillespie, Tracy. Director. Loudoun Museum, Inc., 14-16 Loudoun Street SW, Leesburg, Virginia.

Kilday, Cheryl. Loudoun Tourism Council, 108-D South St. SE, Leesburg, Virginia.

King, John Henry and Susan Farmer. Manager. Town of Leesburg, Economic Development, 25 W. Market St., Leesburg, Virginia.

Kruse, Earl. Business Tek Services, P.O. Box 4344, Leesburg, Virginia.

Richmond, Cynthia, Larry Rosenstrauch, and Robin Bailey. Deparment of Economic Development, 1 Harrison St. SE, 5th Fl., Leesburg, Virginia.

Roberts, Linda. Loudoun Healthcare, Inc., 44055 Riverside Parkway, Leesburg, Virginia.

Smith, Claudia C., Director, Public Relations/Marketing, Columbia Reston Hospital Center, 1850 Town Center Parkway, Reston, Virginia.

Video
County of Loudoun. *Where It's @ Loudoun: The Frontier of InnnoVirginiation.* Leesburg, Virginia: Loudoun County Department of Economic Development. 1999. Focus on technology-related corporations, colleges, universities, and laboratories in the Loudoun area.

Blending Tradition With Innovation

Enterprise Index

America Online, Inc.
22000 AOL Way
Dulles, Virginia 20166
Phone: 703-265-2120
www.corp.aol.com or www.aol.com/careers
pages 78-81

Atlantic Coast Airlines
515 Shaw Road
Dulles, Virginia 20166
Phone: 703-925-6000
Fax: 703-925-6299
Email: rick_delisi@acaicorp.com
www.atlanticcoast.com
pages 86-87

Enterworks, Inc.
19886 Ashburn Road
Ashburn, Virginia 20147
Phone: 703-724-3800
Fax: 703-724-3868
Email: info@enterworks.com
www.enterworks.com
page 89

Foxcroft School
P.O. Box 5555
Middleburg, Virginia 20118
Phone: 540-687-5555
Fax: 540-687-8061
Email: foxcroft@foxcroft.org
www.foxcroft.org
pages 120-121

Galen Photography
P.O. Box 20108
Washington, D.C. 20041
Phone: 703-437-5060
Fax: 703-437-7715
Email: david@galenphoto.com
www.galenphoto.com
page 103

The Holiday Inn at Historic Carradoc Hall
1500 East Market Street
Leesburg, Virginia 20176
Phone: 703-771-9200
Fax: 703-771-1575
Email: leesburggm@crownam.com
pages 126-127

Lansdowne Resort
44050 Woodridge Parkway
Leesburg, Virginia 20176
Phone: 703-729-8400
Fax: 703-729-4096
www.lansdowneresort.com
pages 128-129

Loudoun County Chamber of Commerce
5 Loudoun Street, Southwest, Suite A
Leesburg, Virginia 20175
Phone: 703-777-2176
Fax: 703-777-1392
Email: info@loudounchamber.org
www.loudounchamber.org
pages 110-111

Loudoun County Government
County Administrator
1 Harrison Street, Southeast, Fifth Floor
P.O. Box 7000
Leesburg, Virginia
Phone: 703-777-0200
Fax: 703-777-0325
Email: coadmin@co.loudoun.va.us (main)
good4biz@loudounva.com
   (economic development)
www.co.loudoun.va.us (main)
www.loudounva.com (economic development)
pages 112-113

Loudoun County Transportation Association
P.O. Box 2833
Leesburg, Virginia 20177
Phone: 703-777-2708
Fax: 703-777-2552
Email: loudountranceo@aol.com
page 91

Loudoun Healthcare, Inc.
44045 Riverside Parkway
Leesburg, Virginia 20176
Phone: 703-858-6000
Fax: 703-858-6610
www.loudounhospital.org
pages 116-117

The Loudoun Times-Mirror
9 East Market Street
P.O. Box 359
Leesburg, Virginia 20178
Phone: 703-777-1111
Fax: 703-771-0036
Email: ltmeditor@timespapers.com
www.loudountimes.com
pages 84-85

Loudoun

Merrill Lynch
3 South King Street
Leesburg, Virginia 20175
Phone: 703-779-8006
Fax: 703-779-8756
Email: john_w_sheehan@ml.com
patrick_huge@ml.com
www.ml.com
pages 96-97

The Miles/LeHane Group, Inc.
205 North King Street
Leesburg, Virginia 20176
Phone: 703-777-3370
Fax: 703-777-4861
Email: feedback@mileslehane.com
www.mileslehane.com
pages 98-99

Raspberry Falls Golf and Hunt Club
41601 Raspberry Drive
P.O. Box 590
Leesburg, Virginia 20176
Phone: 703-779-2555
Fax: 703-779-8721
www.raspberryfalls.com
pages 124-125

Reston Hospital Center
1850 Town Center Parkway
Reston, Virginia 20190
Phone: 703-689-9030
Fax: 703-689-0840
Email: claudia.smith@columbia.net
www.restonhospital.com
pages 118-119

Sevila, Saunders, Huddleston & White
30 North King Street
Leesburg, Virginia 20176
Phone: 703-777-5700
Fax: 703-771-4161
page 102

Talbot and Company, Inc.
109 East Market Street
Leesburg, Virginia 20176
Phone: 703-771-8268
Fax: 703-771-7935
Email: helena@talbotandcompany.com
www.loudouncounty.com
www.talbotandcompany.com
pages 100-101

Telos Corporation
19886 Ashburn Road
Ashburn, Virginia 20147
Phone: 703-724-3800
Fax: 703-724-3865
Email: info@telos.com
www.telos.com
page 88

The Town of Leesburg, Virginia
P.O. Box 88
25 West Market Street
Leesburg, Virginia 20178
Phone: 703-771-2734
Fax: 703-771-2727
Email: econdev@leesburgva.com
www.leesburgva.com
pages 106-109

United Airlines
2323 Horse Pen Road
Herndon, Virginia 20171
Phone: 703-326-7754
Fax: 703-572-3926
www.ual.com
pages 82-83

WAGE, AM 1200
711 Wage Drive, South West
Leesburg, Virginia 20175
Phone: 703-777-1200
Fax: 703-777-7431
Email: wage@wage.com
wwww.wage.com
page 92

Washington Dulles International Airport
Metropolitan Washington Airports Authority
1 Aviation Circle
Washington, D.C. 20001-6000
www.mwaa.com
page 90

Index

A

Adopt A Pet program, 54-55
Adult Basic Education program, 60
Agency on Aging, 52
Airmont, 14, 37
Aldie, 13
Aldie Mill, 13
Algonkians, 20
Ambulatory Surgery Center, 67, 117
America Online, Inc., 7, 12, 29, 31, 62, 78-81, 110, 112
American Children of SCORE, 46
Appalachian Trail, 22
Arcola, 13
Arlington, 45, 49, 63
Arts in a Nutshell, 46
Ashburn, 13, 32, 63, 81, 83, 88-89, 131-132
Ashburn Farm, 13
Ashburn Village, 13
Atlantic Coast Airlines, 12, 82, 86-87
August Court Days, 21, 25, 47, 109

B

Ball's Bluff Regional Park, 19, 22, 45, 106
Beaumeade, 32
Birch Hollow, 74-75
Blossom and Bloom, 55
Blue Ridge Mountains, 11-13, 16, 20, 106-107
Blue Ridge Speech and Hearing Center, 53, 69, 102
Bluemont, 13-14, 16, 37, 109
Bluemont Concert Series, 43, 46, 48
Bluemont Country Dances, 46
Bluemont Fair, 13
Bobby Mitchell Hall of Fame Golf Classic, 44
Broadlands, 16

C

C & O Canal, 45
Campbell, John, 20
Cancer Care Center at Countryside, 66
Cascades, 17, 32
Center for Innovative Technology, 29-30, 63
Christmas in April, 54
Civil War, 13-14, 16-17, 19-22, 25, 45, 47, 55, 106-107, 110, 127-128
Classic Car Show, 47-48
Community Connections, 53
Countryside, 17, 66

D

D.C. Metro Area Board of Education Guide, 61
Daily Bread, 52, 56
Daniel Boone in the Old Dominion, 53
Davis, Westmoreland, 23, 47, 69, 84
Department of Economic Development, 28, 91, 103, 112
Department of Mental Health and Mental Retardation, 53
Department of Social Services, 54
Dodona Manor, 23, 108
Draft Horse and Mule Day, 44, 47
Dulles, 7, 13, 16, 23, 27-29, 31-32, 36, 47, 77-79, 85-87, 101, 103, 106, 108, 110, 113, 117
Dulles Greenway, 27-28, 82
Dulles Town Center, 28, 36, 127

E

Echo, Inc., 53
Elder Choices, 52
Enterworks, Inc., 88-89
Ethics Day, 68, 119
Eustis family, 23
Excellence in Education Banquet, 62

F

farming, 11-12, 14, 20-21, 30, 33, 48, 72-73, 75, 84, 113
Fauquier County, 13-14
Field of Flowers, 47
Fife and Drum Corps, 47
fire and rescue volunteers, 55
First Friday Gallery Walk, 36, 109
First Night, 37-38
Fourth of July celebration, 37-38
Foxcroft School, 120-121

Franklin Park, 16
Future Farmers of America, 73

G

Galen Photography, 103
general stores, 14, 37
George Mason University, 29, 63
George Town, 14, 106
George Washington University, 29, 63, 88, 92
GM-YES Program, 62
Godfrey, Arthur, 28
Godfrey Field, 28, 108
Good Shepherd Alliance, 54
Good Shepherd Clothes House, 55
Governor's Magnet School, 59-60
Graydon Manor, 68

H

Hamilton, 13
Harmony, 13
Head Start, 60
Health Information Library, 67
Health Resource Center, 67
Healthy Community 2000, 68
Hechts, 36
Heritage Hall, 69
Herndon, 55, 132
Hillsboro, 13-14
Holiday Inn at Historic Carradoc Hall, the, 126-127
Homes Tour and Craft Exhibit, 17
horses, 14, 30, 44, 46-48, 55, 73, 75, 113, 116, 132
Hospice of Northern Virginia, 67

I

Ida Lee Park, 52, 106
Interfaith Relief, 52, 56, 119, 129
Iroquois, 20

J

JCPenney, 36
Job For A Day, 62
Jones, Robert Trent Jr., 44, 128-129

K

Kids Day, 52

L

Lansdowne and Basin Street Jazz Club, 63
Lansdowne Resort, 12, 127-129
Leesburg, 13-14, 16-17, 22-24, 36, 40, 44, 55, 62, 65-66, 69, 74, 84-85, 90-92, 96-103, 105-109, 113, 116, 120-121, 124, 126-128
Leesburg Corner Premium Outlets, 28, 36-37, 109, 127
Leesburg Executive Airport, 28, 108
Leesburg Flower and Garden Festival, 47
Leesburg Restaurant, 40
Lincoln, 14, 20-21, 25
LINK, Inc., 55
Lord & Taylor, 36
Loudoun Abused Women's Shelter, 53
Loudoun All-County High School Jazz Band, 63
Loudoun Animal Shelter, 54-55
Loudoun Arts Council, 46
Loudoun Association of Retarded Citizens, 53
Loudoun Ballet Company, 43, 46
Loudoun Communities That Care, 54
Loudoun Community Band, 46
Loudoun Concert Orchestra, 46
Loudoun County Chamber of Commerce, 8, 32-33, 81-83, 85, 87, 92, 96, 101-103, 110-111, 117, 119, 124, 127
Loudoun County Day, 46
Loudoun County Department of Parks, Recreation, and Community Services, 54
Loudoun County Government, 30, 112-113
Loudoun County Public School, 61
Loudoun County Transportation Association, 91
Loudoun Education Alliance of Parents, 62
Loudoun Education Foundation, 62
Loudoun 4-H, 44, 51, 73
Loudoun Farms Tour, 45
Loudoun Healthcare, Inc., 65-68, 83, 103, 115-117

Loudoun Hospital Center, 62, 65-67, 91, 116-117
Loudoun, Lord, 17, 20
Loudoun Museum, 24, 107
Loudoun Resolves, 20
Loudoun Restoration and Preservation Society, 21, 25
Loudoun Sketch Club, 46
Loudoun Symphony, 43, 46
Loudoun Therapeutic Riding Foundation, Inc., 53
Loudoun Times-Mirror, the, 84-85
Loudoun Valley, 16, 22, 117
Lovettsville, 11, 14, 20-21, 47, 91
Lowes Island, 17
Lucketts, 14, 41, 44

M

Manahoac tribe, 20
Marion duPont Scott Equine Medical Center, 29, 69
Marshall, George C., 20, 22, 23, 108
Marshall Plan, 23, 108
Marymount University, 29, 63
Mature Worker program, 52
MCI WorldCom, 12, 29, 110
Mellon, Paul, 55
Merrill Lynch, 96-97
Metropolitan Opera, 46
Middleburg, 13-14, 22, 37, 44, 46-47, 55, 100, 120-121
Middleburg Bucks, 37
Middleburg Classic Horse Show, 46
Miles/LeHane Group, Inc., the, 98-99
Monroe Technology Center, 60-62, 67, 117
Monroe, James, 23, 107
Monroe's Practical Nursing School, 62, 67
Morningside, 53
Morven Park, 23, 29, 44, 46, 69, 84, 107
Mosby, John, 22
Mother Net, 67
Mount Weather, 13

N

National Museum of Natural History, 46
National Registry of Historic Landmarks, 36
National Sporting Library, 47, 55
Neale Concert Series, 46
Neersville, 14
New Town, 14

Northern Virginia Brain Injury Association, 53
Northern Virginia Community College, 29, 60, 63
NOVA Urgent Care, 67, 117
NOVA West-Self Help for the Hard of Hearing, 53, 69
Nutcracker, the, 46

O

Oak Hill, 23, 107
Oatlands Plantation, 20, 22-23, 46, 72, 107
Office of Housing Services, 54
Oktoberfest, 47
Old Ashburn, 13
Old Dominion Beer Fest, 44
Orbital Sciences, 29, 62, 110

P

Paeonian Springs, 16
Parents Love A Neighborhood School, 62
Patowmack Farm, 45
Peter and the Wolf, 46
Philomont, 14, 16, 37
Physician Referral, 67
Piedmont Behavioral Health Center, 68
Pink House, the, 41
Piscataway Indians, 14
Player, Gary, 44-45, 125
Poolesville, Maryland, 45, 47
Potomac Celtic Festival, 46-47
Potomac River, 11-12, 14, 19-20, 22, 46, 106-107, 128
Purcellville, 14, 16, 45-46, 49, 67, 84, 117
Purcellville Urgent Care, 67

Q

Quakers, 14, 17, 20-21, 25, 38

R

Raspberry Falls Golf and Hunt Club, 44-45, 111, 124-125, 127
Red Fox Inn, 13
Red Rocks Wilderness Overlook Regional Park, 45
Resourceful Woman, the, 54-55
Reston Hospital Center, 65, 68, 118-119

Retired and Senior Volunteer Program, 52
Rokeby, 23
Roosevelt, Franklin Delano, 20, 23
Round Hill, 16
Rural Economic Development Task Force, 72, 101

S

Sears, 36
Senior CAFEs, 52
Senior Friends, 68
Sevila, Saunders, Huddleston & White, 102
Shenandoah Conservatory Faculty Jazz Septet, 63
Shenandoah University, 29, 63
Smithsonian Institution's Naturalist Center, 46
Snickersville, 13
South Riding, 16
Special Olympics, 53
Sporting Art Exhibit and Sale, 47
Sterling, 16-17, 55, 63, 66-67, 82-83, 117
Strayer University, 29, 63
Summer Job Match, 54
Sunrise Assisted Living Centers, 53, 66, 68

T

Talbot and Company, Inc., 100-101
Tarara Winery, 44
Taste of the Towns, 47
Tax Preparation Assistance Program, 52
Taylorstown, 17, 21
Telos Corporation, 12, 62, 88, 110
Temple Hill Farm Regional Park, 45
Thomas Birkby House, 74
Time Travelers, 24
Title V, 52
Town of Leesburg, 20, 23, 28, 40-41, 56, 106-109
Transcendental Arts Council, 46
Transitional Housing Shelter, 54
Treaty of Albany, 20
Trevor Hill Plantation, 74-75

U

U.S. Navy Band, 46
United Airlines, 12, 82-83, 86-87, 103, 110
Uran, Irwin Wayne, 55

V

Very Special Arts-Loudoun County Theatre Troupe, 53
vineyards, 29-30, 44, 75, 128
Virginia Center for Innovative Technology, 29-30
Virginia Cooperative Extension, 54
Virginia Foxhound Club Hound Show, 44, 47
Virginia Historical Society, 55
Virginia Tech's Regional College of Veterinary Medicine, 56, 69

W

WAGE, AM 1200, 92
Washington and Old Dominion Railroad, 13, 38, 44
Washington and Old Dominion Railroad Regional Park and Trail, 44, 49
Washington Dulles International Airport, 13, 16, 23, 27, 29, 31, 47, 77-79, 82, 86-87, 90, 106, 110, 113, 126, 128
Washington, D.C., 12, 16, 22, 27, 48, 80, 83, 91, 98-99, 106, 110, 120, 128
Waterford, 16-17, 20-21, 25, 38, 41, 54-55, 74, 96
Waterford Concert Series, 46
Waterford Foundation, 17, 96
Waterford Village, 41
Westmoreland Davis Memorial Foundation, 69
Wheatlands, 74
White's Ferry, 47, 106
Whitehall Estate, 23
wine, 29-30, 32, 46-47, 73, 109
Women's Resource Center, 54
Women's Shelter, 51, 53-54, 121

X

Xerox, 12, 62

Y

Young Parents Network, 54

Photos on pages 2, 4, 6 and the dustjacket by David Galen.